A Practical Guide to
ETF Trading Systems

Anthony Garner

January 2010

To Freddie and Aubyn

Hope you enjoy it and
perhaps even profit from it!

Lots of love

Ant

HARRIMAN HOUSE LTD
3A Penns Road
Petersfield
Hampshire
GU32 2EW
GREAT BRITAIN

Tel: +44 (0)1730 233870
Fax: +44 (0)1730 233880
Email: enquiries@harriman-house.com
Website: www.harriman-house.com

First published in Great Britain in 2009 by Harriman House.

ISBN 978-1-906659-27-1

British Library Cataloguing in Publication Data
A CIP catalogue record for this book can be obtained from the British Library.

Printed in the UK by the MPG Books Group

Disclaimer

The test results contained in this book represent hypothetical performance based on the use of computerised system logic.

Hypothetical performance results have many inherent limitations, some of which are described below. No representation is being made that any investor will or is likely to achieve profits or losses similar to those shown. There are frequently sharp differences between hypothetical performance results and the actual results subsequently achieved by any particular trading program. One of the limitations of hypothetical performance results is that they are generally prepared with the benefit of hindsight. In addition, hypothetical trading does not involve financial risk, and no hypothetical trading record can completely account for the impact of financial risk in actual trading. For example, the ability to withstand losses or to adhere to a particular trading program in spite of trading losses are material points which can also adversely affect actual trading results. There are numerous other factors related to the markets in general or to the implementation of any specific trading program which cannot be fully accounted for in the preparation of hypothetical performance results all of which can adversely affect actual trading results.

Readers are strongly advised to conduct their own rigorous testing and research before putting any of the ideas or systems described in this book into practice (if at all) and before taking any financial risk.

Contents

Preface

What this book is about

This book is about developing simple, robust, rule-based trading systems of a trend-following nature. It covers the back-testing of rule-based systems and the application of rule-based trading systems to portfolios of index tracking Exchange Traded Funds (ETFs) and Exchange Traded Commodities (ETCs).

Who this book is for

This book has been written for the intelligent investor who has the time and the inclination to investigate rule-based trading and who may wish to pursue the topic further through his own back-testing and system design.

How this book is structured

The book is composed of two parts–

Part 1

- Introduces the concept of rule-based trading by setting out rules and brief test results for a very basic system.

- Gives numerous examples of fund managers who have demonstrated that rule-based trading works in the real world (and not just in theory).

- Describes the tools you need to conduct your own research before putting rule-based trading into practice for your own account.

Part 2

- Establishes a benchmark by which to judge the performance of the systems described in this book, using a buy-and-hold approach on the various different portfolios used in the system back-tests.

- Sets out the rules for two very effective rule-based trading systems: the Bollinger Band Breakout and the Momentum system.

- Contains detailed test results for each system using a number of different portfolios, showing what the application of such rules to past market data would have achieved by way of investment performance.

Introduction

There has never been a better time to demonstrate the advantages of rule-based investing.

At a time when long only traditionalists are fully invested in stocks and nursing huge losses, the long term systematic trader has exited many markets entirely and waits patiently for a signal to re-enter. The losses he has suffered are likely to be far less severe.

This book reflects my informed belief that successful investing is not complex and that the investor should spurn traditional, actively managed funds run by professionals (which are by and large an expensive waste of time) in favour of managing his own investments.

This book will demonstrate that using a rule-based trading system is likely to provide far better risk-adjusted returns than conventional approaches.

Part 1

Rule-based Trading

A Simple Mechanical System

The aims of this chapter are–

- To introduce rule-based trading with an example of a very simple mechanical system, which sets out exact rules as to when to buy and when to sell a security. (More complex systems will be introduced in Part 2 of this book.)

- To test the efficacy of the system as measured against the benchmark of a buy-and-hold approach.

A basic rule-based system

The rules

Let us take a rule-based trading system of extreme simplicity. Here are the rules:

1. **Entry:** When the closing price of a stock crosses above a *double smoothed* 200-day moving average of the closing price of that same stock, buy the stock at the open the next morning.

2. **Exit:** When the price of the stock closes below the 200-day moving average, sell the stock and remain in cash until another buy signal is given.

Let's look quickly at a few concepts–

- *Double smoothing*: Means taking the 200-day moving average of the closing price and averaging that average over 200 days. Double smoothing makes for a less jagged moving average, which follows the price less closely and helps to remove short-term market noise.

- *Trend following*: This is a classically simple, pure trend following system: the theory is that when prices start to move significantly in one direction, they tend to continue in that direction for a while. All the trader has to do, is to hop on the trend and enjoy the ride while it is going his way and to hop off when his system tells him the trend is over.

- *Cutting your losses*: On many occasions, the trend won't go your way and you have to cut your losses in accordance with your system's rules. The "hopping off" bit is vital: few long term mechanical systems produce more winners than losers. They rely on big winners to overcome the many small losses, so as to come out with an eventual overall profit. This can only happen if losses are cut short while winners are allowed to run.

- *Capturing the middle of the trend*: Trend followers do not expect to be able to buy at the bottom and sell at the top. The lagging nature of their indicators means that they will only benefit from the middle portion of a trend. They buy some time after the market has started to move up and sell some time after the market has started to go down again. This is a fact of life for trend followers.

Does it work?

You will now legitimately ask: does it work? The question can be answered by applying the rules to historical data and by then comparing the results to a buy-and-hold approach applied to the same data.

Rule-based trading test 1: the system applied to the Dow

The following charts and tables represent the growth of starting capital of USD100,000 obtained by applying this simple trend following system to the Dow Jones Industrial Average for the period 1st January 1900 to 4th November 2008.

Ending Balance	CAGR%	MAR	Max total equity DD	Longest drawdown	Trades
24,668,244	5.19%	0.1	50.8%	105.8	295

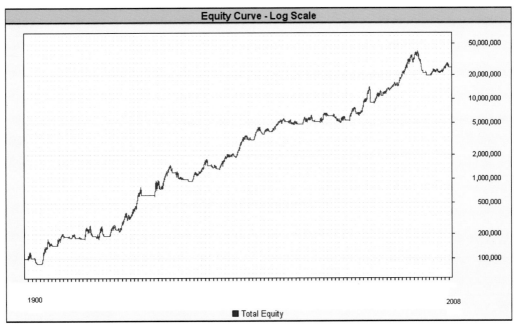

Source: Trading Blox LLC

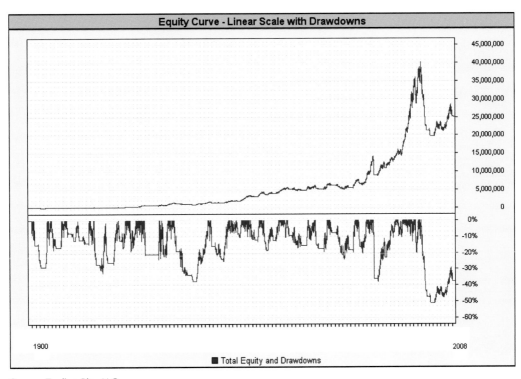

Source: Trading Blox LLC

Trading performance		Win/loss statistics		
Average max drawdown %	37.45%	Wins	50	16.90%
Average max drawdown length	86.22	Losses	245	83.10%
Standard deviation %	12.22%			
		Total	295	100.00%
Total win dollars	45,659,686			
Total loss dollars	21,090,153	Winning months	903	69.10%
Total profit	24,569,532	Losing months	404	30.90%
		Total	1307	100.00%
		Average win dollars	913,193	
		Average loss dollars	86,082	
		Profit factor	2.16	

Points to note

A few notes on the preceding analysis–

- **CAGR**

  The test shows that the system as applied to the Dow Jones Industrial Index over the period of 108 years would have turned initial capital of $100,000 into $24.7m, representing a modest compound annual growth rate of 5.19%.

- **Number of trades**

  The system produced a total of 295 trades. Just under three trades a year, so a reasonably long-term system.

- **MAR ratio**

  This ratio is an often used "pain to gain" ratio and was developed by the Managed Accounts Review for ranking Commodity Trading Advisors. It is calculated as follows:

  MAR Ratio = CAGR / Max Total Equity Drawdown

  In other words how much pain (how big a loss in your account) are you willing to put up with to achieve the gain (the theoretical compound annual rate of return).

- **Maximum total equity drawdown**

  This is a one time event and represents the largest retracement relative to an equity high in the entire simulation: in this case the maximum loss of account equity after a previous high was 51.1% and occurred during the market downturn earlier this decade (June 2003 to be exact).

- **Other drawdowns**

  The "underwater" (or drawdown chart) indicates that the next worst drawdowns in terms of severity occurred in November 1988 (37.53%) and October 1941 (37.48%) while the Wall Street Crash of 1929 caused a mere 20.84% decline for this system. A closer inspection of the system's trades reveals that in 1929 the system exited the market on 25th October 1929 and remained out of the market until April 1933. By contrast, during the worst drawdown for the system, which took place earlier this decade, the system faced the worst possible conditions for trend following: the price crossed and re-crossed the moving average losing money on each trade. In a later chapter we will discuss some possible methods for reducing damage in choppy markets.

- **Length of drawdown**

  It is important to note the length of the longest drawdown: 105.8 months. This is the maximum length of time between succeeding equity highs. Many stock market investors at the moment will be wondering how long they will have to wait before they see the highs they reached on their investments in October 2007. As it happens, the longest drawdown for this system on this index began in early 2000 and is still in progress.

- **Additional statistics**

  Spare a moment to look at the additional trading statistics and win/loss statistics. They serve to emphasise the nature of this system:

- **Volatility**

  Note the volatility or annualised standard deviation of monthly returns of 12.22%; many use this as a proxy for risk – the lower the figure the lower the risk.

- **Win/loss ratio**

  The vast majority of trades lose money (83%). However, as a result of running winners and cutting losers, the average winner is over 10 times the average loser in dollar terms and an overall profit ensues.

- **Dollars won/lost**

  In overall terms, this makes for total dollars won of $45.7m – more than twice the amount of total dollar losses ($21m) and resulting in an overall profit for the period of $24.6m and a profit factor of 2.16 (total dollar profits/total dollar losses).

- **Assumptions**

  Note the following assumptions made for the purposes of this test:

- **Dividends**

  The data used for this test was "price only" data which does not include the effect of re-invested dividends. This makes a considerable difference to index performance, since the dividend yield on the US market averaged almost 4% for much of the past century. Profits would have been a lot higher if a total return price series had been used.

- **Earned interest**

  I did not include interest earned on capital while out of the market – this too makes a considerable difference.

- **Brokerage/slippage**

  I made no allowances in this test for brokerage costs or for slippage – each entry was assumed to have been made at the exact opening price for the index on the relevant day and each exit was assumed to have been made at the moving average.

- **Management fees**

  No deductions were made for management fees or other expenses. An ETF tracking the Dow would be subject to such expenses.

Establishing a performance benchmark

Buy and hold

In order to make a fair judgement on the performance of this basic system, it must be compared against what an investor might have expected to receive on a buy-and-hold basis. In other words, if an investor bought the DJI price index in January 1900 and held it until 4th November 2008 what return would he have made (excluding dividends) and what drawdown would he have suffered? The same assumptions are used as for Ruled Based Trading Test 1 above.

The charts and data tables below give us the answer.

Rule-based trading test 2: buy and hold on the Dow

Ending Balance	CAGR%	MAR	Modified Sharpe	Annual Sharpe	Max total equity DD	Longest drawdown	Trades
14,120,339	4.65%	0.05	0.34	0.08	89.20%	302.8	1

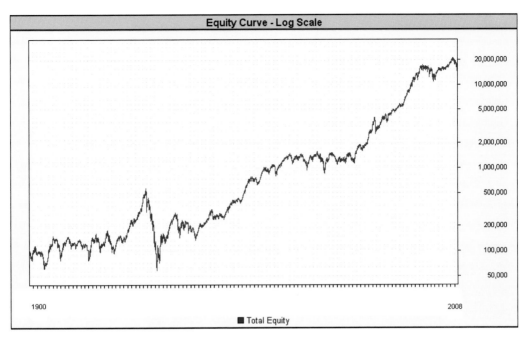

Source: Trading Blox LLC

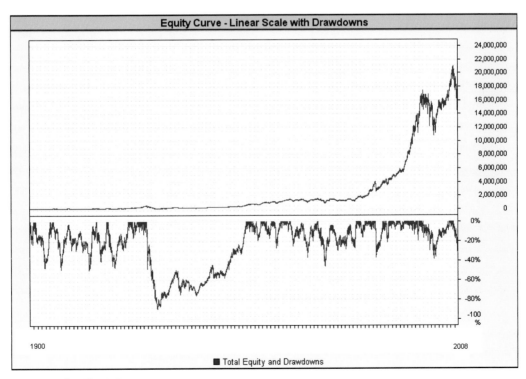

Source: Trading Blox LLC

Trading performance		Win/loss statistics		
Average max drawdown %	55.09%	Wins	1	100%
Average max drawdown length	142.14	Losses	0	0%
Standard deviation %	15.04%			
		Total	1	100.00%
Total win dollars	14,020,339			
Total loss dollars	0	Winning months	750	57.74%
		Losing months	557	42.60%
		Total	1307	100.00%

The comparison table set out below enables a clear view to be taken as to whether the system manages to improve upon the performance of the buy-and-hold benchmark.

Comparison Table

	System	Buy and hold
CAGR	5.19%	4.65%
Risk adjusted CAGR	5.19%	3.06%
Max total equity drawdown	50.8%	89.20%
Average max drawdown	37.4%	55.09%
Longest drawdown	105.8 months	302.8 months
Average max drawdown length	86.22 months	142.14 months
Standard deviation %	12.22%	18.57%
Winning months	903	750
Losing months	404	557

Comparing absolute CAGR

That the system's absolute CAGR happens to be higher than that of buy-and-hold is incidental: research shows that a simple system such as this usually matches rather than betters the return of a buy-and-hold approach over time.

Comparing risk adjusted CAGR

It is customary when comparing investments to standardise returns at the same risk level. When two investments have the same returns, the rational investor will choose that with the lowest risk. Likewise when two systems have the same risk, the rational investor chooses that with the highest return. To reduce the risk (standard deviation) of buy-and-hold above to the level of that of the system, divide the higher risk of 18.57% by the lower risk of 12.22% giving 1.52. Now divide the CAGR of buy-and-hold by 1.52 giving a much lower risk adjusted return of 3.06%. The rational investor would choose to invest in the system rather than the buy-and-hold approach.

Comparing maximum drawdown

As the above table demonstrates, the system's maximum drawdown is almost half that of the buy-and-hold alternative. While a peak to valley loss of 50.8% is indeed steep, it is a great improvement on 89.20%.

Comparing longest drawdown

After the 1929 crash a buy and hold investor had to wait 25 years before he regained the pre-crash peak. The longest drawdown for the system during this test period is "only" just under 9 years.

Comparing risk

Since the system spends a lot of the time out of the market, its risk or volatility (annualised standard deviation of monthly returns) of 12.22% is 34% lower than that of the buy-and-hold investment (18.57%); that is a great improvement.

Comparing winning months

The system had a positive performance in 69% of the months of this long test while the buy-and-hold investment achieved a positive performance in only 58% of the months.

Summary

- A simple mechanical system provides far superior risk adjusted performance to that of the buy-and-hold alternative.

- A system provides more gain for less pain.

- A rational investor would choose (taxation aside) to invest using a mechanical system rather than a buy-and-hold approach.

Does Rule-based Trading Work in the Real World?

The aims of this chapter are–

- To reassure the reader that rule-based trading is a reality and not simply the theoretical output of computerised back-testing.

- To provide references to real world fund managers who have used mechanical strategies to generate impressive profits for many years.

- To provide references to academic research which supports the inescapable conclusion that rule-based trading works.

The background

Sceptics and practitioners

Most traditional fund managers, the long only stock pickers, scoff at the very idea of being able to profit from simple mechanical systems which exploit observed market phenomena such as momentum and trends. It is a fact however that many hedge funds and Commodity Trading Advisors have profited handsomely from such strategies over the past three decades, which seems reason enough to give credence to such systems, or at least not to write them off without serious investigation.

The academics

Many academics who point out the underperformance of the mutual fund industry are adherents of the efficient market hypothesis and claim that the only proper way to invest is passively – by tracking and remaining long an index. Broadly, the efficient market hypothesis claims that financial markets reflect in their prices all known information and that it is not possible therefore to outperform the market except by chance. Other academics however have produced interesting studies in support of the notion that timing *can* enhance the investment process.

Backtesting

My own extensive back-testing strongly suggests that market timing techniques can be usefully combined with index funds to produce risk adjusted returns which are superior to a buy-and-hold strategy. And certainly superior to the performance of most mutual funds.

Caveat

The reader should bear in mind that my conclusions are by definition based on interpreting past performance (covering, usually, a maximum period of around 30 years) and what has worked in the past may not necessarily hold good in the future. Emphasis on the word "necessarily": I suspect that simple timing strategies will continue to perform well, especially if watched carefully and updated on a periodic basis in line with changing market conditions.

Rule-based fund managers

Evidence from the real world

The market place provides irrefutable evidence that rule-based trading strategies have been profitably employed over long periods of time by real life money managers. Many of the fund managers mentioned in this section apply rule-based systems to the futures markets rather than to cash equities or funds (ETFs or otherwise) but the broad principles are similar whichever instrument they are applied to.

Renaissance Technologies

Discarded the discretionary approach

Mathematician James Simons' Renaissance Technologies is an interesting place to start, although hard facts are difficult to come by unless you are an investor in his funds.

James Simons began his investment career as a discretionary investor, using his own judgement, as do the vast majority of traditional fund managers. By the end of the 1980s he had turned to quantitative models and lost interest in fundamental analysis. He is quoted as saying–

With old fashioned stock picking, one day you feel like a hero. The next day you feel like a goat. Either way, most of the time its just luck.

The Medallion Fund

According to their marketing material, they–

approach investing largely as a scientific problem that human acumen, advanced mathematical and statistical methods, and robust technology are well suited to address.

Simons' Medallion Fund has achieved 39% compound annualized returns net of huge fees from 1989 through to 30th June 2007 and according to press reports continued to perform at similar levels in the taxing environment of 2008. A report on Bloomberg at the end of November 2008 quoted Medallion as being up 58% for the year to date.

REIF

Medallion was closed to outside investors a while ago and a new fund, the Renaissance Institutional Equities Fund was launched, to invest in US equities on a long/short quantitative basis. It is generally understood that the fund uses different techniques from Medallion and trades longer term; certainly, its track record so far is a lot less glamorous. As of 30th June 2008 the retail tranche of a fund run by RIEF for Société Générale Asset Management, net of fees and in US dollar terms, had achieved an annualised return of 1.7% since inception (September 2006) with volatility of 7.99% and a maximum peak to valley drawdown of 18.42%. On all measures except volatility, thus far RIEF has slightly underperformed the S&P 500 but it is perhaps rather too early to draw much of a conclusion.

Tactical Investment Management Corporation

Background

Tactical Investment Management Corporation and its founder David Druz provide a useful lesson in the long term viability of trend following strategies. His website can be found at www.tacticalnet.com and it is highly recommended reading. Tactical is a registered Commodity Trading Advisor (CTA) and Commodity Pool Operator in the US with a track record in following trends in the futures markets stretching back to 1981.

Track record

From its inception on 1st July 1981 up to the end of August 2008, Tactical's Commodity Trading programme achieved a compound annual rate of return of 17.8% while the Institutional Programme which started in 1993 achieved 18.8%. In terms of risk, the institutional programme suffered a maximum peak to valley drawdown during this period of 30.75% and records an annualised standard deviation of monthly returns of 25.14%.

Purely systematic

Tactical's method of trading is purely systematic and all trading decisions are made by following computer driven algorithms which give buy and sell signals over the widely diversified portfolio of futures it trades.

Inefficient markets

In sharp contrast to the believers in an "efficient market", Dr Druz believes that his trading is profitable because of the exact opposite: he considers that the futures markets are not efficient and that trends in price can be distinguished and exploited. If a market is moving, his computer driven system will have him hop on the trend and follow it up (go long) or down (go short).

The Turtles

Trading places

Many will be familiar with the famous trading experiment where Richard Dennis and William Eckhardt successfully taught rule-based futures trading to a group of individuals who have become known as the "Turtles". Many of the original Turtles subsequently became successful systems based fund managers in their own right.

Track record

Eckhardt Trading Company's record for its standard programme goes back to 1987, with an annualised compound return of 26.4%, an annualised standard deviation of monthly returns of 39.82% and a maximum peak to valley drawdown of 29.08% as of the end of September 2008.

The IASG database

Further track records

The IASG database at www.iasg.com contains the track records of many other successful futures based systematic trend followers dating back as far as 1977 including the following (as of end September 2008):

Manager	Start date	CAGR%	Max DD%	Volatility
Millburn Ridgefield Corporation – Diversified Program	1977	13.96	33.47	21.07
Campbell & Company – Financial, Metal and Energy	1983	13.04	41.92	19.76
John W Henry – Financial and Metals	1984	21.65	43.60	37.70
Dunn Capital Management – World Monetary Assets	1984	14.02	57.66	35.86
EMC Capital Management Classic Program	1985	25.11	45.35	51.78
Mark J Walsh & Co – Standard Program	1985	23.57	43.04	40.82
Abraham Trading Company	1988	21.32	31.96	34.47
Chesapeake Capital	1988	14.74	23.36	21.25
Hawksbill Capital Management	1988	24.99	61.78	51.18
Saxon Investment Corporation – Diversified Program	1988	16.12	41.55	26.05
Rabar Market Research – Diversified Program	1988	13.90	29.84	23.02
S&P 500	1980	9.02	46.28	14.73

Academe

Theoretical background

You may think it redundant to look at academic research when an assessment of some of the real life fund managers out there tells us that momentum strategies work. Not so, I would argue. An additional bonus of digging into the research is that it gives us a theoretical background as to why such techniques work. The two papers referred to below are examples of the very extensive research available for free on the internet.

"Momentum" (Jegadeesh)

An article entitled "Momentum" written in October 2001 by Narasimhan Jegadeesh of the University of Illinois and Sheridan Titman of the University of Texas is freely available for download from the website of The Social Science Research Network (SSRN).

The paper cites substantial evidence that stocks that perform the best (worst) over a three to twelve month period continue to perform well (poorly) over the subsequent three to twelve months and that momentum trading strategies which exploit this phenomenon have been consistently profitable in the US and most developed markets. This conclusion is of particular relevance to the Momentum System set out in Part 2 of this book.

A number of possible reasons for the phenomena are discussed and while no firm conclusions are drawn, the paper makes interesting reading. Most explanations would seem to detract to a greater or lesser extent from the efficient market hypothesis. The possible (and largely unconfirmed) explanations include the theory that stocks initially under-react to information and continue to move as investors digest the implications over time.

"Market Timing Strategies That Worked" (Shen)

Pu Shen, an economist at the Federal Reserve Bank of Kansas City wrote an interesting paper in May 2002: "Market Timing Strategies That Worked". He points out that *market timing* is a loose expression and that many commentators doubt that it is ever a viable investment strategy. By contrast, his back-testing of some simple strategies suggests that profit is to be had, and many different systems are out there to be tested.

Pu Shen concludes from the back-testing outlined in his paper that four out of the five strategies he proposes outperformed the market index (the S&P 500) in the sense that they provided higher returns at lower risk than the market, even allowing for transaction costs.

To quote–

Our research suggests that it may be possible to use a simple rule of thumb to avoid some of the market downturns and to improve upon the widely preached buy and hold strategy.

He uses data from 1970 to 2000 and his focus is on the spread between the earnings to price ratio of the S&P 500 and interest rates. The earnings to price ratio is the inverse of the more familiar price earnings ratio and the interest rates used were the three month Treasury Bill rate and the ten-year Treasury Note rate.

The theory tested was that there may be times when the stock market is so expensive in relation to bonds that it is better to get out altogether. The test portfolio switches between the stock market and cash using the spread between the earnings to price ratio of the stock market and the relevant interest rate for a signal. Put very simply, the signals tell you when the stock market looks too expensive against short-term bills or longer-term bonds: when it does, the system switches you out of the stock market and into cash. When better value is to be had, the system switches you back into the stock market.

As to why his system worked, Pu Shen came to the conclusion that it kept out of the stock market in periods where inflation was a major problem for the economy and thus the stock market.

Summary

- There are many successful and publicly available real life track records which demonstrate that rule-based trading is profitable and works in the real world.

- There are academic studies which provide theoretical support for the efficacy of rule-based trading.

- The diligent investor applying some simple rules of thumb on a systematic basis to financial instruments of his choice, can hope to achieve performance at least as good as, if not better than, the majority of products currently offered by investment professionals.

Back-testing: Data

The most important task a prospective rule-based investor should undertake is to back-test his proposed strategies.

In order to back-test, the investor must obtain sufficient and accurate historical data for the instruments he intends to trade.

The aims of this chapter are–

- To emphasise the importance of obtaining historical market data going back as far as possible.

- To show the impact of dividends on overall return and to stress the need to obtain dividend data for stock indices.

- To explain the elements of commodity investment returns and the need to build commodity indices for back-testing.

- To help the reader overcome some of the frustrations he will encounter and to point in the direction of possible data sources.

Taking a long-term view

ETFs are very new instruments. Barclays Global Investors were the first to come up with a range of index tracking products on a wide variety of global markets but these funds were only launched in 1996.

But anyone who has been in the financial markets a while will know that it is a mistake to look at a mere decade or so of price data. To see why, let's re-visit a very long term chart of the Dow Jones Industrial Index:

The Dow Jones Industrial Average 1897 to 2008

Source: Equis International

As you can see from the preceding chart, there have been times over the past 120-odd years when the US stock market has had devastating downturns. As you can also see, there have been long periods of time when the market has gone nowhere.

We will now take a closer look at shorter periods within the past 120 years of US stock market history.

The object is to emphasise that a prospective investor who wishes to be brutally realistic, must base his expectations for future returns on a very long-term view.

After reading this section, I hope you will find it hard to look at mutual fund advertisements touting fabulous five-year track records without some scepticism.

Back-testing test 1: the Dow January 1980 to January 2000

Picture yourself as a prospective US investor in January 2000 with the ability to obtain reliable daily data on an index tracking fund following the Dow and going back to January 1980. Twenty years of data; not bad you might think. And indeed, the results below look most promising for a buy-and-hold strategy on the Dow for this period.

End balance	CAGR%	MAR	Sharpe	Ann Sharpe	Max TE DD	Longest drawdown	Trades
$1,321,718	13.78%	0.39	0.95	0.90	35.7%	24	1

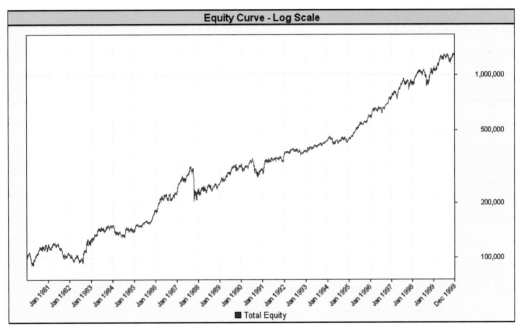

Source: Trading Blox LLC

Key points to note

- **CAGR** of 13.78% for this period is a very attractive return.

- **Maximum drawdown** of "only" 35.7% is not severe by historic standards.

- **Longest drawdown** was a mere two years – 24 months.

- Re-investing **dividends** would add to the performance. These figures were calculated on a price index only;

Oh happy the investor who actually achieved this performance!

But how short-sighted of the prospective investor, conducting his due diligence in January 2000, to rely on only 20 years of past data for forecasting future returns.

To see why, let's take a look at what happened during a few other 20 year periods. Let's see whether today's investor might be grateful to be forewarned that investing in the stock market is not always such plain sailing.

Back-testing test 2: the Dow January 1962 to January 1984

Below I have set out the performance our luckless investor would have achieved buying and holding the Dow for the period 1st January 1962 to 1st January 1984, which tells an altogether sorrier story.

End Balance	CAGR%	MAR	Sharpe	Ann Sharpe	Max TE DD	Longest drawdown	Trades
$162,072	2.44%	0.06	0.24	-0.03	44.2%	117.8	1

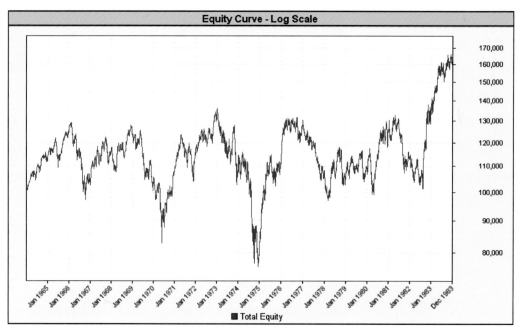

Source: Trading Blox LLC

Key points to note

- **CAGR** of a miserable 2.44% (excluding dividends).

- **Maximum drawdown** of 44.2% – making for a dismal 0.06 MAR pain to gain ratio.

- **Longest drawdown** of almost ten years to regain the peak in account equity seen at the beginning of 1973.

Let's take a look at another couple of 20-year periods.

Back-testing test 3: the Dow January 1909 to January 1929

Here are the results for the period 1st January 1909 to 1st January 1929: it turned out all right in the end but the first 14 or 15 years of going nowhere can not have been much fun.

End Balance	CAGR%	MAR	Sharpe	Ann Sharpe	Max TE DD	Longest drawdown	Trades
$339,433.75	6.30%	0.14	0.43	0.13	45.9%	82.1	1

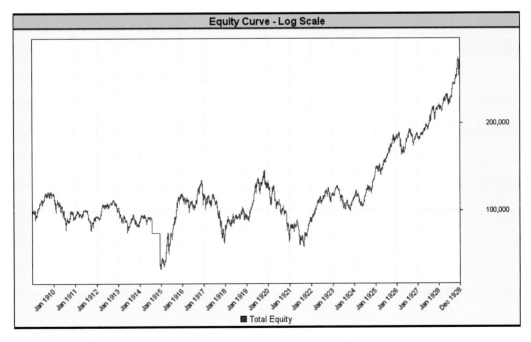

Source: Trading Blox LLC

Key points to note

- **CAGR** of 6.3% which is in line with the very long-term performance but all of that return was achieved in the last five years or so.

- **Maximum drawdown** of 45.9% – making once again for an unattractive pain to gain ratio.

- **Longest drawdown** just under seven years from peak to peak. A long time to wait for your money back.

Back-testing test 4: the Dow January 1929 to January 1950

How about investing in the Dow just before the Great Crash? Here are the results from buying and holding through the period 1st January 1929 to 1st January 1950. Not a very pretty picture.

End Balance	CAGR%	MAR	Sharpe	Ann Sharpe	Max TE DD	Longest drawdown	Trades
$57,932	-2.69%	-0.03	0.04	-0.21	89.20%	232.1	1

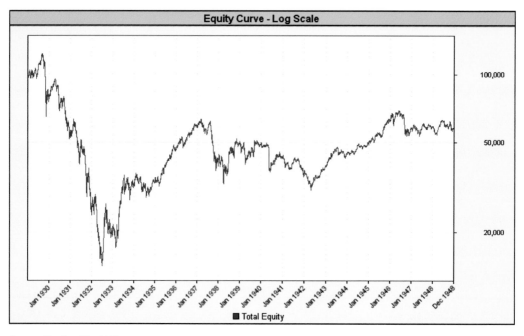

Source: Trading Blox LLC

Key points to note

- **CAGR** of -2.69%. Excluding dividends you would have lost 42% of your original investment during this 20-year period.

- **Maximum drawdown** of almost 90%.

- **Longest drawdown** 19 years. You would never have reached the peak seen in 1929 during this 20-year period (in price terms, excluding dividends).

Conclusion

- There is only a very short period of price data available for ETFs.

- Obtain the longest history you can secure for stock indices as a proxy for index tracking ETFs.

- There have been long periods in stock market history where equities have been a frustrating investment.

- Long periods of desultory stock market performance may occur again in the future.

Data suppliers for equity indices

I have made my point: you need as much historical data for as many different markets as you can lay your hands on. You are going to have to rely on stock index data since ETFs are new instruments with a short price history.

Now for the disappointment: this sounds easy enough but the task is actually a nightmare.

Bloomberg/Reuters

If you want to spend the money subscribing to Bloomberg, Reuters or the like, maybe the task becomes easier. I don't. Certainly if you are an investment bank you are likely to want to buy very long-term data from somewhere, assuming you don't already have it.

Stock exchange websites

Private investors could start by taking a look at the Hong Kong Exchange's website (www.hkex.com.hk); where I think you will begin to get the picture. Once you start getting to the detail, you will find that the data is patchy, awkward and/or expensive.

And you will encounter similar problems when you look at each exchange website.

Reference books

How about a book? Surely there must be some grand tome containing all the information you need? I was sent a link where I could search online in a book with the promising sounding title *The International Guide to Securities Market Indices* written by Henry Shilling. To my delight, the book contained at least annual dividend information for even the most obscure of stock indices. Unfortunately, the book only starts its data in 1985 and ends in 1996; the book does not seem to have been re-published since.

End-of-day data feeds

There are data vendors who provide reasonably accurate end-of-day historic data for reasonable prices over a wide range of markets. At the end of each trading day you simply download the day's prices and your software updates your stream of historic data for you.

By far the best I have come across to date is CSI Data (www.csidata.com). I have used CSI's data for both futures and stocks and have been very happy with the product.

If, despite my warnings, you are happy to use a mere 10 or 12 years of data then subscribe to CSI and use their data for Barclays Global Investor's range of index tracking New York listed ETFs. You will not be displeased with the results. CSI proficiently adjust their data for splits, bonus issues, consolidations and so forth and even provide you with the ability to access two price streams: one unadjusted price stream so you can see the actual price of the stock as it traded on the day and the other, the back adjusted price.

The need for back adjustment

Even the greenest investor is likely to understand the need to adjust historic stock and index levels for corporate actions and the like. Take a stock which today closes at $1 and tomorrow finalises a ten-into-one consolidation: tomorrow the stock opens at $10; of course the overall capitalisation of the company and its market value remain the same. It is window dressing by the management. As an investor who held 10 stocks with a market value of $1 each you now hold instead one share valued at $10. So, the stream of prices needs to be adjusted by multiplying by 10 every price prior to the consolidation. If the stream of data was not so adjusted, your back-test would erroneously assume a huge profit when it sees the stock apparently jump from $1 to $10.

Stock dividends

For an extra payment, CSI will also let you split out a list of actual cash dividends paid out by these funds so that your testing can simulate a total return investment. You get a list of dividends paid and you can ask your clever back-testing software to simulate re-investment of these cash dividends at intervals which makes sense to you: quarterly or bi-annually perhaps.

Dividend data for stock indices

Stock index dividend data difficult to obtain

Neither CSI, nor any other data supplier I have so far been able to find, provide dividend data for stock indices. Some, including CSI, produce a few total return indices but no one seems able to provide you with a list of cash dividends. Total return indices will do for our purposes but it is better by far to have the cash dividends listed separately so that you can make the choice of if, when, and how you want to simulate dividend re-investment.

Do dividends matter?

Yes, they matter very much indeed and assuming dividend re-investment gives a huge boost to index returns.

Set out below I detail the difference quarterly dividend re-investment makes to a buy-and-hold investment of USD100,000 in the Dow Jones Industrial Index for the period 1st January 1900 to 4th November 2008.

Here are the figures with and without dividend re-investment:

Back-testing test 5: the Dow with and without dividends

	Ending balance	CAGR%	Max total equity DD	Longest drawdown
No dividends	14,120,339	4.65%	89.20%	302.8
Quarterly dividend re-investment	2,155,107,249	9.60%	85.3%	117.5

As you can see, the addition of cash dividends and the assumption of quarterly re-investment of those dividends has:

- **doubled the return**; and

- **decreased the longest drawdown period** (post the 1929 crash) from 25 years to just under 10 years.

So, yes, dividends matter very much when looking at stock market returns.

I will leave to the reader the question of whether it would be feasible to re-invest cash dividends in this manner, including such considerations as income tax on dividend receipts.

A practical approach to obtaining dividend data

If neither CSI nor any other reasonably-priced data supplier provide index dividend data, how does the investor obtain the information?

The answer is by a combination of methods:

- Combing very thoroughly through the web for available information.

- Buying relevant books (Standard and Poor's have a compendium which gives dividend data for S&P indices).

- Fudging the issue. You may be able to obtain dividend data for the Dow Jones Wilshire 5000 for instance but not for the Russell 3000; you may consider it a legitimate fudge to apply the percentage dividend rate obtained from the former against the price index levels of the latter.

I fully admit that I have had to rely liberally on such fudges for my own index data and I firmly believe that it is better to have an imperfect approximation of dividends, than to base one's assumptions on price data alone.

Dividend data may be reasonably easily found for major indices but less easily for more exotic markets.

Long-term stock index data hard to come by

Pre-1980 data

Unfortunately, it is remarkably difficult to obtain daily data for almost any stock index in digital form, from a reasonably priced end of day data provider, reaching much further back than 1980.

You can obtain *monthly* closing prices for longer periods, but while monthly data does a good job in giving you a broad picture for a buy and hold investment, it is more than a little misleading for testing systems, unless you are content to assume entering and exiting markets at the close at monthly intervals only.

MSCI Barra

Monthly data will greatly underestimate volatility and draw-down. But if you are content with this, you can download monthly data for free for a wide range of MSCI indices, going back to 1969, on the MSCI Barra website (www.mscibarra.com).

CSI (Commodity Systems Inc.)

As I write, I am looking at a database of daily stock index data available from CSI. The longest price series available is the Dow Jones Industrial Average which goes back to 1928, followed by the S&P 500 going back to 1950.

So far so good, but the most important ingredient to long-term investment success is diversification, and CSI's offering on non-US indices is unappealing.

The MSCI World Index is available from 1972 but thereafter it gets very scrappy with the next longest dated price series being the Nikkei 225 starting from 1984.

Equis International

The other provider I have used is Equis International (www.equis.com), a company now owned by Reuters.

Apart from the Dow Jones Industrial Index (first data point: 2nd January 1897) and the MSCI World (first data point 1st January 1976) I can find no country index data commencing earlier than 1980.

I find the Equis data download software user unfriendly and the company were unable to provide me with a list of their index coverage and start dates.

Reuters

I considered buying data from Reuters itself but since Equis tell me their data is supplied by Reuters, I wonder whether Reuters would be able to provide me daily data going back any further. In any case, the person I spoke to at Reuters also claimed they were unable to provide me a list of what indices they covered and from what start dates.

Global Financial Data

One interesting source of very long-term data is Global Financial Data (www.globalfinancialdata.com). I have not tried their data and it is very expensive but I glean from their website that they are able to provide both price and dividend data going back for long periods. For instance I see that they will provide the UK FT Actuaries Dividend Yield from 31st December 1923 to 18th November 2008 and also the UK FTSE All-Share Index from 1693 to 2008!

Apart from price, there are other aspects of the data which (to me at least) fall short of the ideal. On the FTSE All Share, daily data is only available back to 1968 prior to which it is either monthly or weekly. Also of course, since neither the Financial Times nor the FTSE All Share Index existed in 1693, GFD have had to add their own extension. Fudges and approximations are a fact of life in terms of data availability. We have to make do with what we can get.

Standard & Poor's

Talking to S&P, they pointed out to me that one major problem has been the digitisation of data (or the lack thereof). Much of the daily price information can probably be obtained (at least back to around 1970) but a lot of it is only available in written form. Still, I do find it odd that 1970 is now considered ancient history.

Making do

If the only century-long stream of data you can obtain is that for the DJI, it is still a whole lot better than nothing. It tells us that even in a century of enormous technological and economic growth (albeit punctuated by the two world wars) stock markets go nowhere for long periods but that in the long term the rewards are there.

Commodity data

The need to construct your own commodity indices

Exchange Traded Commodities (ETCs) present the analyst with an equally difficult task in terms of data. ETCs in general use an investor's money to take positions in the futures markets, although a few buy physical product where appropriate or feasible. Since the trading history of ETCs is so very short, the diligent back-tester must construct his own indices of futures price movements as ETC proxies, making sure to include all three elements of the return to be gained in the futures markets.

Elements of return in commodity futures

The three elements of return are as follows:

* **price** return,
* **roll** return,
* return on your **collateral**.

Let's look at each of these in turn.

Price return

Price return is obvious – if you buy 1 futures contract in January for delivery of 1,000 barrels of crude oil in March at a price of $50 per barrel, and the price has increased to $55 per barrel by the time you come to sell your position in mid-February, you will make a profit of $5 per barrel, or $5,000.

Roll return

Roll return is rather more subtle. A long-term investor in futures has to keep rolling over his positions in the futures markets, since futures contracts expire during or prior to the relevant delivery month.

Roll return is either positive or negative:

* **Positive**. Where the near month contract (March by way of example) trades at a higher price than the next contract month (April in our example) the market is said to be in *backwardation* and the roll return for a long only investor will be positive.

- **Negative.** If the reverse is true the market is said to be in *contango* and the roll return for a long only investor will be negative.

I give brief explanations of *backwardation* and *contango* below.

Backwardation

Take crude oil: at the open of floor trading on 2nd January 2008 you go long 1 contract of March 2008 crude on NYMEX, which obliges you to take delivery of 1,000 barrels of crude in March 2008 at a cost of $97.85 per barrel.

Since you can't actually accommodate 1,000 barrels of crude in your bathtub, you must roll the contract into the April 2008 contract before the March contract ceases trading on 22nd February 2008.

So, on 11th February 2008 at the opening of the trading pit in New York, you sell your March 2008 contract at 91.90 and buy the April 2008 contract at the lower price of 91.85.

You have made a large loss on you purchase and sale of the March contract of $5.95 per barrel or $5,950 in total.

As you can see however, you have sold March at a slightly higher price than you had to pay for April and so have made a small profit on the roll.

Roll profits can form an important element of total return for a long only investor in a market such as crude which has, historically at least, often been in "backwardation".

Contango

Many markets such as gold and grains tend to trade in contango. The higher price you may have to pay for further out contracts (April trading at a higher price than March) is often explained as a substitute for the insurance and storage you would have to pay were you investing in the physical product.

Return on collateral

A speculator in the futures market would not have had to put down the full purchase price of $97,850 for his 1,000 barrels of oil when he took his position on 2nd January 2008 – he would only have put down a deposit or margin of around 10% of the full contract value.

ETCs however tend to be fully collateralised: an investor who wanted exposure to 1,000 barrels of crude on 2nd January 2008 would have to invest around $97,850 in buying shares of an ETC which tracks the price for crude oil.

ETC sponsors don't have very big bathtubs either: it is not very convenient to have to store large quantities of crude oil and so sponsors use the futures market instead.

In simplistic terms, the sponsor of the ETC uses 10% of your purchase price ($9,750) as a margin deposit to buy 1 contract of Crude Oil and he invests much of the balance in short-term cash investments, usually short term US Government Treasury Bills.

The return on this cash is used to pay the fund's costs and any balance will accrue to the fund itself. Hence the *collateral return.*

Further explanation

All this will not be easy for a newcomer to the futures market to absorb. The most helpful suggestion I can make, is that the reader who finds my explanation difficult to follow, or who wants to expand his understanding turns to the internet. Download the relevant prospectus for a few different ETCs from a few different providers and also take a look at the way Total Return Commodity Indices are calculated. A particularly helpful publication is *The Dow Jones-AIG Commodity Index Handbook* which I was able to download for free.

As I warn elsewhere in this book, while the basic concepts of investing are far from difficult, and the systems I propose in this book are simple in the extreme, the devil is in the detail. The more work you put in, the greater your understanding.

In the next chapter I make mention of Trading Blox backtesting software. In the forum open to purchasers and users of that software, I placed a piece of coding which forum members can use to generate commodity indices from interest rate and commodity data.

Data accuracy

The importance of data accuracy is the final point to make in this chapter. Erroneous data will make a nonsense of back-testing.

In my experience, CSI's data is relatively clean and the company are very keen to keep it that way. They seem to comb it thoroughly, presumably using computer algorithms which alert them for abnormally large opening gaps or daily ranges or any of the other factors which can creep in and suggest erroneous data.

I set out below a few charts derived from Equis data which I reported as erroneous. Unfortunately I have to say that the apparent errors were numerous but on the more positive side, Equis were keen to correct an error if such it transpired to be.

Here is a chart of the Chilean Stock Exchange Inter 10 index; if uncorrected, such data can give alarming results in a back-test:

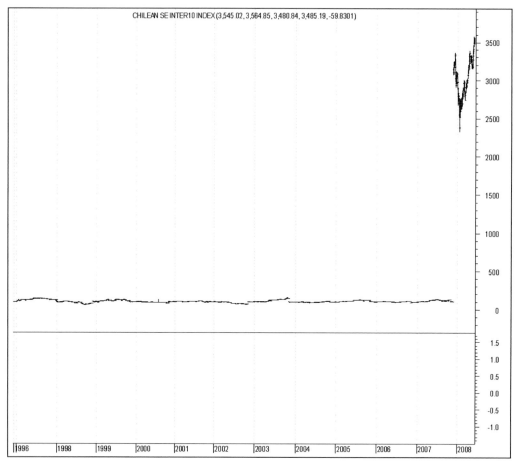

Source: Equis International

Here is an unfortunate chart of the Istanbul Stock Exchange IMBK 100 Index:

Source: Equis International

And the Sao Paulo Stock Exchange IBX Index:

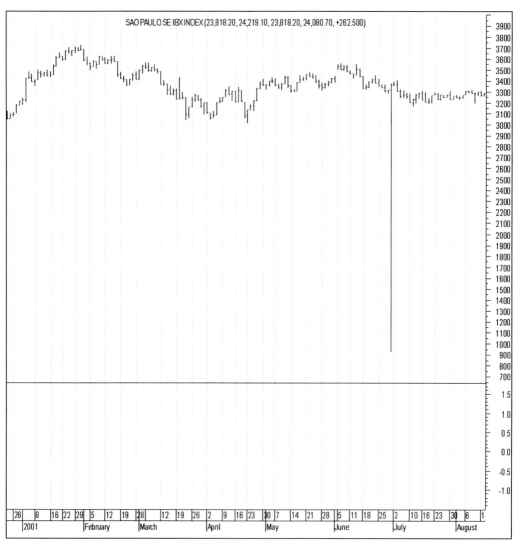

Source: Equis International

Here is an interesting one (the Madrid Stock Exchange General Index) which I queried and which turned out to be correct: apparently, the index was annually re-based to 100 each year from 1940 to 1986. Clearly, in back-testing, one would only wish to use correctly back adjusted data so as to iron out the non-existent 40% drop in the index market capitalisation in January 1985.

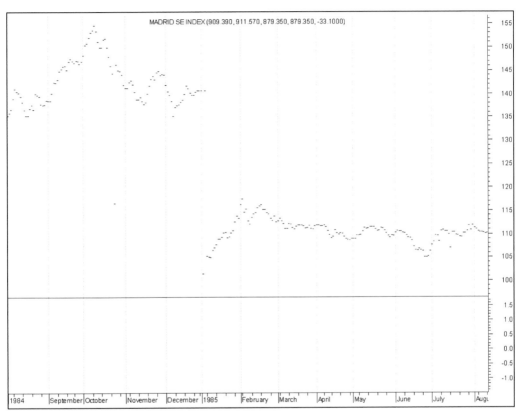

Source: Equis International

Summary

- Obtaining appropriate and accurate market data is the first essential step towards back-testing rule-based trading strategies.

- Compromise on data quality and length is likely to be a necessity for those without very considerable resources in both time and money.

Back-testing: Software

The aims of this chapter are–

- To introduce high end back-testing software.

- To introduce products that I have used in my own research and trading.

- To outline some of the more important features you should look for in purchasing back-testing software.

The need for sophisticated software

Anyone seriously interested in rule-based trading should invest in a full featured and sophisticated back-testing engine.

A back-testing engine is a software application that runs simulations of trading rules over historic financial market data. It determines what trades would have been executed on the basis of those rules and what profit or loss would have resulted. If your proposed rules are such that you can describe them to a computer, and you have the relevant data, then you can test any system your imagination can come up with.

Some software solutions

Trading Blox

I have used software called Trading Blox in my back-testing since its inception by ex-Turtle Curtis Faith back in 2003 (www.tradingblox.com). Tim Arnold, the current proprietor, has improved the software enormously since its already very good earlier versions.

Trading Recipes

Prior to that point I had used Trading Recipes which has now morphed into Mechanica (www.mechanicasoftware.com).

I have found both Trading Blox and Mechanica to be excellent but it is down to the prospective purchaser to conduct a thorough review of the market as a whole and to decide what product best suits his purpose.

All back-tests and related graphs, tables and figures used in this book were produced by Trading Blox.

Do not resent the cost of back-testing software and do not compromise by buying an inferior product. Your investment of a few thousand dollars will be repaid many times over in the knowledge, skill and experience you will gain. And hopefully in trading profits.

Software features

Many assume that they can back-test using Excel or some relatively low cost and readily available spreadsheet package. You *can* but it is a poor substitute. To put it in perspective, a friend of mine, whose background is in computer science and programming, helps run a small hedge fund. It took him seven years to build his now excellent back-testing software.

Trading Blox (or its predecessor Veritrader) has taken some years and much input from users to grow into the superb product available today. My strong advice therefore would be not to be a cheapskate.

Typically, low end software masquerading as a back-testing programme will only be able to execute simple trading rules on single instruments in a single base currency.

What can a product like Trading Blox or Mechanica do for you?

High end back-testing software will have features along the following lines

- **Portfolio level testing**. You can test an entire portfolio of multi-currency instruments in one test and the results will be expressed in a base currency of your choice.

- **Suite level testing.** You can test a suite of different systems each using a different portfolio of different instruments and the detailed results will be given for the combined test as well as per system.

For instance you may wish to take total starting capital of $1m and devote 50% to trading a moving average crossover system on a basket of 100 blue chip stocks from different world markets, 20% to buying and holding a portfolio of multicurrency bonds and the remaining 30% to a Turtle style breakout system on a diverse basket of 80 world futures contracts.

- **Built in systems.** The software should include a generous number of ready to run built in systems to get you started, particularly if you are new to writing computer code. Some software will even come with sample data so that you need not waste money on a subscription before you are ready to trade.

  You can use the coding of the built in systems to learn the ropes and will soon find you have the ability to adapt and alter the coding to express the individual ideas you wish to test.

- **Data comparison.** The product should have the ability to read one set of data and compare it in a test against another set.

  You may wish to have access to the S&P 500 index data for instance to use as a filter: only go long a stock or ETF if the S&P is trading above its 200-day moving average.

- **Fully programmable software.** You need the ability to test your own ideas; don't buy software which *only* lets you test one or more pre-programmed systems.

- **Realism.** Make sure that the software enables a wholly realistic basis for testing.

  Does it allow you the flexibility to include commissions and if so on what basis? Will it calculate interest on any balance of your capital sitting in cash rather than invested in stocks? Does it allow you to simulate leverage? Can it implement volume constraints – you may decide you wish to refuse trades where the average daily volume is less than 250,000 shares or perhaps $500,000 in value terms.

- **Parameter stepping.** The software should allow for parameter stepping: the best software will allow you to run a test which shows you the results of allowing a range of parameters to be stepped through and tested one increment at a time in a single test.

  For a dual moving average crossover system for instance, you should be able to test different parameters of each of the long and short moving average in a single test run. You could choose periods for the short moving average of 50 to 100 days in steps of 10 and 150 to 300 days for the long moving average in steps of 20.

  Or you might wish to step any other parameter: the test start date, the duration of the test, the amount of starting capital used, the commission or slippage, or the volume constraints.

- **Report output.** The report output should be comprehensive and include an impressive array of test statistics or even the opportunity to add your own custom devised measures. And you should be able to export as much of the information generated as possible to a spreadsheet format for further analysis.

- **Users' forum.** A well attended users' forum is extremely helpful – an online meeting place where users can exchange ideas, systems and snippets of code. And of course dedicated support from the software provider and a commitment to regular upgrades and corrections of bugs and glitches is essential.

Summary

- It will pay you many times over to buy the best testing package you can afford.

- Its worth may not be immediately apparent to you but over the months and years, you will come to realise just what a valuable and flexible tool you have bought.

Back-testing: Strategy and System Design

The aims of this chapter are–

- To dispel the myth that successful system design is one of the deeper secrets of the universe.

- To set out some basic guidance to those new to system design.

Do I need to be a genius?

Many ask "Do I need to be a rocket scientist to succeed at mechanical systems trading?" The answer is "No."

Anybody with a statistical or applied science background will have a big head start. Even those without such an advantage however, can easily teach themselves basic computer programming from scratch (certainly within a program like Trading Blox or Mechanica). Those with an arts background will certainly benefit from brushing up their maths and basic statistics.

> You do not need any high level capabilities for the simple trend following strategies described in this book: you can test and trade perfectly effectively (and profitably) with basic skills.

Time and effort required

Simple as the concepts contained in this book may seem, the time and effort that need to be devoted to the matter are considerable. The harder you work the more the insight you achieve; your back-testing complements your trading and vice versa.

As the months and years roll by, continued effort yields satisfying "aha" moments (as long-term systems trader Ed Seykota puts it) when suddenly this or that seems to drop into place and make sense.

The learning process is one of a few years before you begin to feel completely comfortable that you know what you are doing.

Avoidance of curve fitting

Curve fitting

The generally perceived wisdom in system design is that "simple is best". The reason usually given is the danger of curve fitting your design to the set of historical data you are working with.

The more rules your system contains, the greater the danger that you are fitting your system to the available data so as to produce a pleasing looking back-test. While working admirably on past data, a curve fit system is unlikely to achieve its real object of making you money in the future.

To take a highly contrived example, look back at the chart of the Dow. You would rightly conclude that exiting all long positions in equities at the beginning of October 1929, October 1987 and October 2007 would have been very beneficial to your pocket book. Lots of other downturns began around October.

To include a rule in a system to exit the market on 1st October in those years and to re-enter a year or two later would make the results look very good in a theoretical back-test but such a rule may not be so effective in keeping you out of future market declines.

Unscrupulous systems sellers have used such techniques in the past to make otherwise hopeless systems look good. The usual routine is to add rules affecting a small number of trades, which conveniently wipe out periods of unprofitable trading, or alternately create huge and unrealistic profits.

Use as much data as possible

Apart from exercising restraint in adding rules it is helpful, when seeking to avoid over fitting, to test your proposed system against as much data as possible over as many different time frames as possible.

Your back-tests should produce many, many trades over many years of data from many different instruments. Cast you eyes back over the chapter on data and take another look at the long-term chart of the Dow. Had you only tested the 20 years from 1980 to 2000 you would have achieved a very lopsided view of long-term market performance.

Test all market conditions

See how your system copes with the long flat periods or the many precipitous drops before making up your mind on its goodness or otherwise. As has already been emphasised, long term daily data is very hard to come by for almost any market but the least you can do is to test your system against many different markets for such periods for which you can obtain data. Stock markets are highly correlated nonetheless, you will find that different markets have tended to behave differently, even if downturns and upturns tend to occur at roughly the same periods.

Predictive value of tests

The more data you use and the more trades you simulate, the more chance that your back-test will have some predictive value for future profitability. If your system can survive and profit in a back-test over many different periods of boom and bust and glum sideways movement, in almost every market from US equities to live cattle, then you might be onto something.

Portfolio testing

Don't get too hung up on individual market performance – overall portfolio performance is more important. Live cattle may not be profitable to trade or hold overall, but might just produce a zig when another component throws up a zag and the combination may well act to smooth your overall returns.

The more markets you test the more realistic you will become in your hopes. The more markets you actually trade, the more chance you have of achieving a reasonably smooth performance.

Don't skimp

The avoidance of data fitting and the discovery of a robust system can only result from intellectual honesty and endless testing and observation. Don't pull the wool over your own eyes and don't skimp on the work and effort involved.

Optimisation

Test different parameters

Do not confuse optimisation with curve fitting.

You should not be afraid of optimising the parameters or rules of your system. Don't restrict yourself to looking at a 200 day moving average: try 5, 10, 15 or 20 days. Try 300 days, or 400. You are likely to find a broad area of results, within the different parameter runs of a system, which provide relatively pleasing performance and your best bet is to choose parameters somewhere within this broadly successful range.

Optimising the basic system

Using the basic system described in Chapter 1, I set out below an example of system optimisation and the interpretation of a stepped parameter test. You will remember the rules of the basic system:

1. When the closing price of a stock crosses above a *double smoothed* 200-day moving average of the closing price of that same stock, buy the stock at the open the next morning.

2. When the price of the stock closes below the 200-day moving average, sell the stock and remain in cash until another buy signal is given.

Using Trading Blox to optimise

Using the parameter stepping facility of Trading Blox, I ran a single test on the Dow Jones Industrial Index from 1st January 1900 to 4th November 2008 using moving average lengths starting at 50 days and increasing by 50 days for each successive test up to 600 days. The results are set out below together with a chart which graphs the CAGR against the length of moving average used. Starting capital was $100,000.

Back-testing test 6: optimising the moving average system

Stepped parameter summary performance

Test	Close average (days)	Ending balance	CAGR%	Max total equity DD	Longest drawdown	Trades
1	50	2,009,090.77	2.79%	78.00%	166.9	699
2	100	4,494,884.35	3.56%	69.20%	143.6	465
3	150	7,193,152.08	4.00%	67.00%	129.3	352
4	200	7,347,640.02	4.02%	64.40%	157.1	295
5	250	5,345,273.21	3.72%	58.70%	154.1	226
6	300	2,185,224.25	2.87%	69.50%	241.2	256
7	350	2,556,574.86	3.02%	57.60%	251.5	221
8	400	2,704,168.46	3.07%	59.90%	307.9	186
9	450	2,828,370.70	3.12%	63.30%	307.6	181
10	500	3,697,076.70	3.37%	56.90%	251.5	147
11	550	1,521,562.18	2.53%	66.30%	298.8	200
12	600	2,533,210.96	3.01%	60.20%	258.5	182

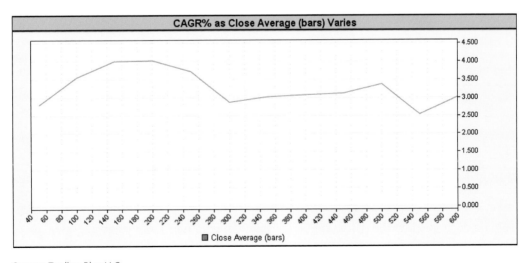

Source: Trading Blox LLC

Interpretation of results

First of all notice that *all* moving average lengths from 50 right through to 600 days were profitable, suggesting that a moving average system is a robust strategy profitable over a very wide range of parameters. The use of a 200-day moving average seems to be in the right sort of ballpark – around the optimum area, at least so far as CAGR is concerned. The duration of the longest drawdown and the severity of the maximum drawdown, also look to be reasonably favourable also for this length of moving average. A 200-day moving average is not a freak or chance result: it sits within a very wide area of profitable parameters.

Time windows

It is important to run tests on different time chunks of the data. A 200-day moving average might look a reasonable "best" length overall, but how did its performance compare with a shorter or longer term moving average in the first decade of the 20th century? And the first decade of the 21st century? Is there any significant difference or trend in profitability of the different length moving averages for these different time periods? You need to seek answers to these questions.

Using realistic assumptions

Trading has frictional costs

You may have noticed that the statistics for the 200-day moving average test above are lower than that for the test on the same data for the same period for the same system set out in Chapter 1. The reason is that the earlier test included no estimate for the costs of trading; this test does.

Higher frequency trading, higher costs

In back-testing it is essential to include a reasonable estimate of the costs of doing business. Trading costs work to the detriment of a system which trades more frequently. The entry and exit costs will be minimal for a buy and hold investment lasting 108 years but far more significant for a system which trades the same instrument several hundred times during the same period.

Transaction costs

So, for the above test I have assumed that a brokerage fee is payable of 0.3% by value of the stock bought and sold and that slippage will amount to 10% on each trade.

Slippage explained

A stock may start trading first thing in the morning at $100 but if you are dealing in an OTC market like NASDAQ, there is no official opening price as there is on the New York Stock Exchange, and you might pay or receive more or less than $100 for your stock bought or sold around the opening. Trading Blox allows you to estimate slippage and add or deduct it to or from your purchase or sale cost.

In the case of a long entry, Trading Blox calculates the range from the theoretical entry price of $100 to the high of the day ($120 by way of example), applies the percentage slippage you specify (10% in this case) and adds it to the purchase cost.

So, in this example if the opening price at which you hope to buy is $100 and the high of the day is $120, the difference of $20 will be multiplied by the 10% slippage estimate to add an additional $2 to the fill price. The adjusted fill price of $102 is then increased to 102.31 by the addition of the 0.3% brokerage commission.

Where to start

Where do you begin?

Many books make a meal over the whole process and there is much hand wringing over the horrible difficulty of coming up with something that works. Many books also come up with enormously and unnecessarily convoluted ideas that will leave you scratching your head and wondering if you are, after all, stupid. But if simplicity is the answer, then why bother with such nonsense?

Long-term trend following

The area this book concentrates on is long-term trend following and it is basically very, very simple indeed to design a robust and straightforward system, which has a sporting chance of maintaining its profitability into the future. Happily, for the long-term trend follower, there are many simple methods of establishing when a trend starts and ends. Design is not complex.

The humble trend follower has a fairly simple task of designing a method which works and there are many tried and tested systems, a few of which you will find in this book.

More complex strategies

Branch out

When you think you understand trend following, experiment with other systems (at least in back-testing and system design). You may or may not find a method of trading and investment which suits you better but your level of understanding and expertise will certainly increase in leaps and bounds.

If you want to investigate counter trend or mean reversion systems, if you want to look into defining and trading on more complex patterns, if you want to look at taking arbitrage trades or spreads then you may need to put in rather more effort.

Sources of ideas

In his excellent tome *Trading Systems and Methods* writer and trader Perry Kaufman gives you enough ideas to test out for the rest of your natural days: pattern recognition, financial astrology, the Elliot Wave Principle, seasonality and cycle analysis. It's all there. Books and magazines are also an excellent source of ideas to test as are online forums such as that run by Trading Blox.

Use your imagination

Be bold, inventive and innovative. If convention has it that you should buy on a given signal and go long, run a test to see what happens if you do the reverse and go short. If conventional wisdom says don't trade this or that instrument, test it out for yourself and see what the results look like.

Take each and every idea and system you come across and experiment with each and every parameter; turn it upside down, inside out; pull it to pieces and put it back together again. I have heard it reported many times that this or that trader has stumbled on a good idea by accident or error – it has certainly happened to me.

Ongoing research

Changing markets?

Research and development are tasks which never end. Some maintain that markets don't change; I take a different view. What worked yesterday or 50 years ago may not necessarily work in 5, 10 or 50 years time. Financial markets seem to become increasingly volatile as the passage of time brings in more players, and this has never been truer than with enormous influx of highly geared hedge fund money over the last decade.

Given the financial collapse and de-leveraging, the game may change yet again. You should constantly test and re-test your methods to see whether they are holding up under current market conditions. Don't hurry to make a change to a tried and tested system but be aware that changes may eventually prove necessary.

Evolution

A prime example of the necessity to evolve is an excellent system first marketed by a well-respected developer back in the 1990s. An envelope was placed around a moving average to filter out whipsaw trades and the system was highly lauded for some years.

As markets seemed to change, profitability dropped and the developer added other filters to ensure that the system only took trades in the direction of a longer-term trend than that captured by the system's moving average. The system still works very well indeed but on different parameters to those originally suggested.

Money management

A much discussed topic

Whole books have been written on the topic and many have claimed (almost certainly erroneously) that good money management can change a losing system into a profitable one.

Try Googling "betting systems" or Martingale or Anti Martingale, or the name Ralph Vince. Unfortunately, complex systems of money management are more relevant to futures trading and gaming than to un-geared trading or investment in ETFs and ETCs.

Put simply…

Don't bet the ranch.

Translated into ETF investing that amounts to diversification, knowing when to exit a trade and not putting all your eggs into one basket. I will revert to the question in later chapters.

Summary

- Time and effort rather than genius are required to develop profitable trading systems.

- Profitable long-term trend following systems are easy to develop.

- Simplicity and the use of a wide range of data over a wide range of time frames are the best protection against curve fitting.

- Research and system design should be viewed as an on-going process.

Part 2

Developing a Rule-based System

Establishing Benchmarks

The aims of this chapter are–

- *Benchmarks* – To establish buy and hold benchmarks against which the success or otherwise of mechanical systems trading can be judged.

- *Diversification* – To demonstrate the benefits of diversification within asset classes.

- *Asset allocation* – To demonstrate the benefits of the addition of other asset classes to stock investment.

- *Standalone commodity investment* – To explore the returns available from long-term standalone investment in commodity ETCs.

Asset allocation and diversification

Asset allocation determines return

Successful investing is largely a matter of asset allocation and diversification, not picking individual investments (let alone individual stocks). Asset allocation is about making a broad decision as to which diversified asset classes to invest in, and this will be the most important determinant of your return. Most of the major asset classes are now available in ETF form: world stocks, world bonds, currencies, commodities, property.

ETFs are the tool of choice

ETFs provide even the smallest investor with enormous diversification, in two forms: diversification across asset classes (in the hope that if stocks are down, at least one other asset class might be up); and diversification away from single stock risk. Few investors can afford the wide spread of individual global stocks and other assets necessary to achieve worthwhile diversification without the use of funds.

An investor holding 20 stocks would lose a significant percentage of his capital if his holdings turned out to include Lehman, AIG, Fortis, or any other formerly highly rated stock which turns out not to be the crock of gold the market formerly assumed. Using ETFs, an investor can spread his risk across hundreds, if not thousands of stocks.

Portfolios of ascending diversification

I have chosen to test portfolios of increasing diversification in ascending order to demonstrate the benefits which accrue. The basic system in Chapter 1 was tested on and benchmarked to a buy and hold strategy on the Dow Jones Industrial Index. In this chapter, successive levels of diversification are introduced and asset classes other than stocks are added to the mix. This chapter concentrates on establishing the buy-and-hold return on diversified portfolios and succeeding chapters apply the same progression to two rule-based systems.

The buy-and-hold strategy as a benchmark

Suitable benchmark

My already stated aim in this book is to show how to use simple mechanical systems to improve upon the risk/reward ratios of conventional investing. As briefly touched on in Chapter 1, the most suitable benchmark against which to measure the performance of such systems is the buy-and-hold strategy.

Buy-and-hold – industry standard

The standard benchmark for the fund management industry is the buy-and-hold performance of a relevant stock index. You can not appreciate the value of rule-based systems (or of a traditional managed fund) in a vacuum: you need a benchmark by which you can judge performance. Typically, publicly available managed funds compare their performance to the stock market index most closely related to the relevant fund. A US manager of a large capitalisation US stock fund would very likely use the S&P 500 as his benchmark. Sales literature will show the fund's performance side by side with the performance you would have achieved for the same period by simply buying the S&P 500 at the beginning of the period in question and holding it through to the end.

Each portfolio benchmarked

Throughout this book I compare historical back-tests of a system's performance on my choice of diversified portfolios to what would have been achieved by simply buying that same portfolio at the commencement of the test period and holding it through to the end of the test period. The rest of this chapter will detail the buy-and-hold returns on each of the following diversified portfolios–

1. Buying and holding the MSCI World

2. Buying and holding an equal weighted portfolio of international equities

3. Buying and holding a portfolio of equities, bills and commodities

4. Buying and holding a basket of commodities on a standalone basis

1. Buying and holding the MSCI World

Biggest exposure is to the US

If you are a US-based investor, reasonably adventurous in terms of your equity portfolio, but preferring to keep your equity allocations more or less in line with market capitalisations and with a majority exposure to the US and the US dollar, then the performance of the MSCI World Index shows you what returns you might have expected over the past 30 years. It is one of the most widely quoted indices in investment circles and a benchmark for a great many actively managed global equity funds.

Price and dividend data

The index has been calculated by what is now MSCI Barra (www.mscibarra.com) since 1969. I have been able to obtain daily prices for the MSCI World Price Index in US dollar terms (i.e. no dividends included) going back to 1976 from Equis. You can extrapolate dividend information from the MSCI Barra website; I did so and assumed quarterly re-investment. If you want to use monthly data, you can download monthly closing prices going back to 1969 for the index and many of its components from the website.

Weighted by market capitalisation

The index is market capitalisation weighted and the table below sets out the country weightings as of 30th September 2008. If you were to buy an MSCI World tracker fund today, you might find in 20 years time that the county weightings differ greatly.

No re-balancing

In some ways then, this index provides no "re-balancing". It depends how one interprets the term but if, as a US investor, you decided that you always wanted US Stocks to constitute at least 50% of your stock market exposure, then you would have to buy individual country funds rather than one based on the MSCI World, and re-balance your portfolio periodically yourself. If your US stock market fund sank in value one year, you would have to sell down your holdings in other country funds and buy more of your chosen US fund to keep your exposure to the US at 50%.

Current weightings

MSCI World Index weightings as at 30th September 2008 were as follows:

Country	Weighting
USA	50.22%
Japan	10.15%
UK	9.79%
France	4.85%
Canada	4.52%
Germany	4.08%
Switzerland	3.50%
Australia	2.85%
Spain	1.84%
Other	8.20%

Buy and hold performance

The graphs and statistics set out below establish what an investor would have seen by way of return, in US dollar terms, by holding the MSCI World Index over the past 32 years.

Buy and hold test 1: MSCI World January 1977 to November 2008

End balance	CAGR%	RAR%	MAR	Annual Sharpe	Max total equity DD	Longest drawdown	RSquared
8,335,124	6.87%	9.59%	0.13	0.21	52.9%	79.7	91.74

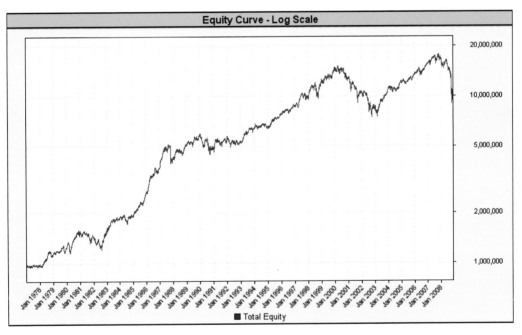

Source: Trading Blox LLC

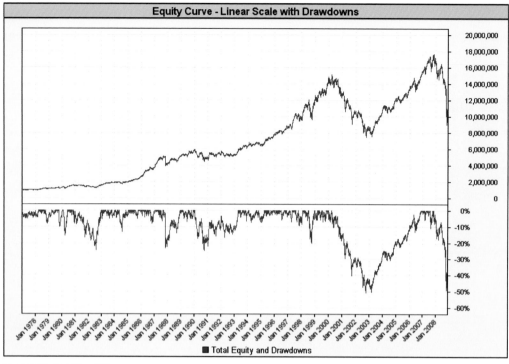

Source: Trading Blox LLC

Assumptions

The assumptions used in all tests in this chapter (apart from differing start and end dates) are as follows:

Parameter	Value
Starting capital	US $1m
Start date	3rd January 1977
End date	20th November 2008
Base currency	US dollars
The assumed Risk Free Rate	3%
Interest	At the rate of three-month US Government T Bills accrues on any un-invested balance
Dividends	Price only indices used but cash dividends are collected and re-invested quarterly
Slippage	Assumed at 10%
Brokerage commission	Charged at 0.3% of the dollar value of the transaction
Total Expense Ratio (TER)	An annual TER of 1.5% is deducted

Performance notes

- **CAGR** – A CAGR of 6.87% may not sound very appealing – three-month US T Bills would have yielded a CAGR of around 5% for the period. But this takes us to the heart of the problem with Buy and Hold.

- **Sensitivity to start and end dates** – The measurement of CAGR on a buy and hold investment is particularly sensitive to start and end dates. The end date of the test is 20th November 2008 – we are in one of the deepest bear markets of the last century. When we come to look at a few simple mechanical systems, we will see that we would have been out of most stock markets by early 2008 and sitting in cash and would thus have recorded a higher CAGR for the period.

- **Choosing a different end date** – It may be an obvious point, but had I ended the test at 20th October 2007, the statistics would have been rather different as follows:

Buy and hold test 2: MSCI World January 1977 to 20th October 2007

End balance	CAGR%	RAR%	MAR	Annual Sharpe	Max total equity DD	Longest drawdown	RSquared
17,067,437	9.67%	9.88%	0.19	0.44	50.7%	79.7	92.04

Main points of note

- **CAGR jumps by 40%** – By moving the test end backwards by a year we have increased CAGR by 40% and made long-term equity investment look far more attractive. A more appropriate guide, I hope, to the future.

- **Regressed annual return** – Take a look at the comparative figures for RAR% (Regressed Annual return); notice that there is very little difference in the figure between the two tests despite the different end dates. Ex-Turtle Curtis Faith, in his excellent book *Way of the Turtle*, suggests that a better and more stable measure of return can be made using a simple linear regression of all the valuations in an equity curve. A linear regression is sometimes called a line of best fit – a straight line drawn through the measurements which the above graph represents. RSquared is in itself a useful measure of goodness for a system and a measure of the straightness of the line of best fit: the higher the number, the straighter the equity curve and the less volatile your investment. RAR is far less sensitive to test start and end dates.

- **Sharpe Ratio** –The annual Sharpe Ratio will be a measure of goodness familiar to most investors: it represents the CAGR (minus the risk free return) divided by the standard deviation of annual returns: the higher the figure, the smoother and less volatile your return.

2. Buying and holding an equal weighted portfolio of international equities

Improving the portfolio: a different perspective

Let's take a look now at what improvements might be made. A long-term trend follower in the futures markets is more accustomed to equal weighting the positions in his portfolio. A futures trader may typically take the same risk on corn as he takes on crude oil or silver. In stock index futures, a speculator will often risk the same amount of capital on the Korean stock market as Japan or the US. It's a very different point of view: many speculators tend to treat all instruments the same, as gambling counters if you like. While successful speculation in the futures market is far from gambling, some of the techniques used are not dissimilar to those of a professional gambler and it does offer a very refreshing and different viewpoint to that of conventional investing.

A 50% allocation to the US?

At the height of the Japanese stock market's glory days, it represented something like 40% of world stock market capitalisation. It now represents around 10%, with the TOPIX index down over 70% from its 1989 high. The US currently represents 50% of current world stock market capitalisation: who knows where it goes from here? My point is, would it have been the right choice to have devoted 40% or more of your assets to the Japanese stock market in the 1980s? Is it the right choice to devote 50% of your stock market allocation to the US in 2008?

Do you think the US stock market and the US dollar will perform so much better than other stock markets and currencies over the next few years? If not, then do you really want to invest five times more in the US than in the UK or Japan? Do you think the UK and the pound sterling will greatly outperform Spain, Italy and Switzerland, the euro and the Swiss franc? If not then do you really want to invest five times more in the UK than in Spain and Italy? Three times more than in Switzerland?

Liquidity constraints

The problem for institutional fund managers running many billions of dollars is that they have little choice. There is simply not the liquidity in the smaller markets to accommodate the enormous sums that they must invest. The private investor is happily in a very different position. If he so chooses, he can achieve maximum diversification and invest equal (or at least more equal) amounts in a wide range of markets big and small.

Rebased test on The MSCI World

I have added an extra statistics box immediately below to show the results of a back-test in identical terms to that above on the MSCI World, with the exception of a new start date to coincide with that of this current test. (This is necessary since regrettably I have been unable to obtain data going further back than 1980 for the constituents of the Equal Weighted Portfolio.)

Buy and Hold Test 3: MSCI World 1st January 1980 to 20th November 2008

Statistics for MSCI World Test with a commencement date of 1st January 1980 and an end date of 20th November 2008

End balance	CAGR%	RAR%	Std dev	Annual Sharpe	Max total equity DD	Longest drawdown	RSquared
6,702,380	6.80	9.12%	15.29	.20	54%	79.9	88.95

Test on equal weighted portfolio

Set out below you will see the results of a back-test which simulates holding equally weighted positions in each of the markets in Portfolio 1, Appendix 1.

Quarterly re-balancing

Equal weightings are maintained by quarterly re-balancing. Because of the varied start dates in Portfolio 1, the test assumes selling down holdings in earlier positions to invest in other markets coming on-stream: this is an example of the unfortunate compromises one must sometimes make when unable to get hold of sufficient historic data. To explain further, my data for the components of this portfolio only start in 1980. In 1980, capital was equally divided between the S&P 500 and TOPIX. In 1981 these two holdings were sold down proportionally to make way for an investment in Taiwan and so on. It does of course warp the results but it also, I hope, gives a reasonably reliable idea of the sort of benefits which might accrue from greater diversification and a different weighting strategy.

Buy and hold test 4: Equal weighted equity indices

Statistics for the Portfolio 1 test with equal weightings with a commencement data of 1st January 1980 and an end date of 20th November 2008

End balance	CAGR%	RAR%	Std dev	Annual Sharpe	Max total equity DD	Longest drawdown	Trades	RSquared
31,733,156	12.70%	15.86%	16.91	0.41	58.9%	45.9	587	95.05

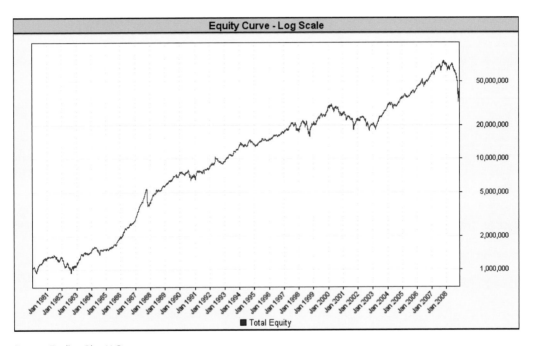

Source: Trading Blox LLC

Source: Trading Blox LLC

Additional assumptions

- Any margin arising eliminated by sale of stock

- Re-balance threshold: 5%

- Buffer of 3% deducted from proposed investment amount to account for stock price movement between previous close and next day's open.

Comparison table

Set out below is a comparison table of the above two tests for easy reference:

	MSCI World	Equal weighted
CAGR	6.80%	12.70%
Risk adjusted CAGR	*6.80%*	*11.48%*
RAR	9.12%	15.86%
Risk adjusted RAR	*9.12%*	*14.34%*
Max total equity drawdown	54%	58.9%
Longest drawdown	79.9 months	45.9 months
Standard deviation %	15.29	16.91
R squared	88.95	95.05

Points to note

Greater diversification seems to have worked its magic:

Trade individual country funds

It is usually the case that trading the individual components of an index separately (rather than trading the index itself) brings benefits even though the constituents are relatively highly correlated. Regardless of weighting, investors are likely to find a better return trading separate ETFs for each market rather than trading a single MSCI World ETF.

CAGR

Even after adjusting the CAGR of the Equal Weighted Portfolio downwards (so as to bring its slightly higher risk in line with that of the MSCI World) greater diversification has achieved an increase of close to 70% in the return.

RAR

Risk adjusted RAR has been improved by 57%.

Maximum total equity drawdown

Maximum drawdown on the Equal Weighted Portfolio has increased by 9% – not a great cost considering the dramatic increase in return.

Longest drawdown

Notice that the longest drawdown is greatly reduced in the Equal Weighted Portfolio.

Standard deviation

This figure represents the annualised standard deviation of monthly returns, the most commonly used indicator of risk in the fund industry.

3. Buying and holding a portfolio of equities, bills and commodities

Now let's add some diversification across asset classes.

Weightings

In this test a 20% weighting is given to three-month US Government Treasury Bills, 20% to commodities (Portfolio 2, Appendix 1) and only 60% to equities (Portfolio1, Appendix 1).

Re-balancing

Re-balancing is undertaken quarterly and takes two forms. As between asset classes, each quarter bills, commodities and equities are re-balanced to maintain the 20/20/60 split. Within the commodities allocation, each commodity is re-balanced each quarter so as to maintain equal exposure to each commodity within the commodities portfolio. Within the equities allocation, each country index is re-balanced each quarter to maintain equal exposure to each index in Portfolio 1.

Buy and hold test 5: equities, bills, commodities

Statistics for the test with a commencement date of 1st January 1980 and an end date of 20th November 2008 are as follows

End balance	CAGR%	RAR%	Std dev	Annual Sharpe	Max total equity DD	Longest drawdown (months)	Trades	RSquared
16,027,453	10.07	11.60	10.50	0.47	40.8%	44.6	6693	95.57

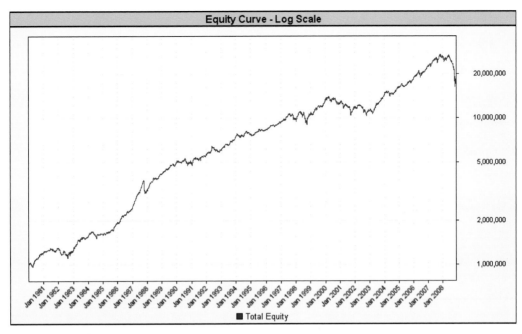

Source: Trading Blox LLC

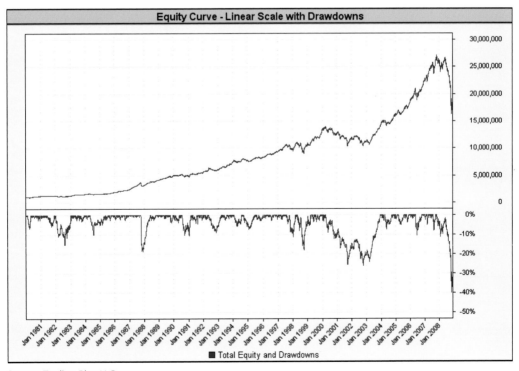

Source: Trading Blox LLC

Additional assumptions

- Any margin arising eliminated by sale of stock

- Re-balance threshold: 5%

- Buffer of 3% deducted from proposed investment amount to account for stock price movement between previous close and next day's open.

- Commodity indices include roll yield and collateral yield.

Comparison table

Set out below is a comparison table of the results for the three portfolios so far tested in this section:

	MSCI World	Equal Weighted	Stocks/Bills/Commodities
CAGR	6.80%	12.70%	10.07%
Risk adjusted CAGR	*4.67%*	*7.89%*	*10.07%*
RAR	9.12%	15.86%	11.6%
Risk adjusted RAR	*6.26%*	*9.85%*	*11.6%*
Max total equity drawdown	54%	58.9%	40.8%
Longest drawdown	79.9 months	45.9 months	44.6 months
Standard deviation %	15.29	16.91	10.50
RSquared	88.95	95.05	95.57

Points to note

The following are the principal points of interest arising from a comparison of test statistics of the three portfolios:

CAGR / RAR

In absolute terms, the return for this more diversified portfolio is substantially lower than that of the Equal Weighted Equities portfolio.

Standard deviation

Note the significantly lower risk profile achieved by the addition of bills and commodities. The lowering of risk is also enhanced by quarterly re-balancing: it is a form of profit taking. Higher performing asset classes in any particular period are cut back (profit is taken) and re-distributed to the lesser performers.

Risk adjusted return

Dividing the higher risk of the Equal Weighted Equities test (standard deviation of 16.91) and the MSCI World test (standard deviation 15.29) by the lower risk of the Stocks/Bills/Commodities test (standard deviation of 10.50) gives us 1.61 and 1.46 respectively. Applying these adjustments to the absolute CAGR and RAR of the earlier tests shows us that after adjustment for risk, the addition of bills and commodities has actually produced a higher return than that of the Equal Weighted Equities portfolio.

Maximum total equity drawdown

Note the considerably lower maximum drawdown of the stocks/bills/commodities mix: the addition of the extra asset classes has achieved more risk adjusted gain for less pain.

4. Buying and holding a basket of commodities on a standalone basis

Dull

Buy-and-hold, long-only investing in a basket of commodities *on a fully collateralised basis* is not exciting. It is the combination with equities which results in a lower risk (standard deviation) and a better risk adjusted return as (in the past at least) one or other component of the combined portfolios goes up as another goes down, thus smoothing the combined performance.

Buy and hold test 6: commodities only

Test of Portfolio 2, Appendix 1, Commodities only, quarterly re-balancing. Statistics for the test with a commencement date of 6th July 1982 and an end date of 20t November 2008 are as follows (later start date reflects lack of data)

End balance	CAGR%	RAR%	Std dev	Annual Sharpe	Max total equity DD	Longest drawdown (months)	Trades	RSquared
4,109,423	5.50%	5.92	10.96	0.19	43.5	49	1707	92.16

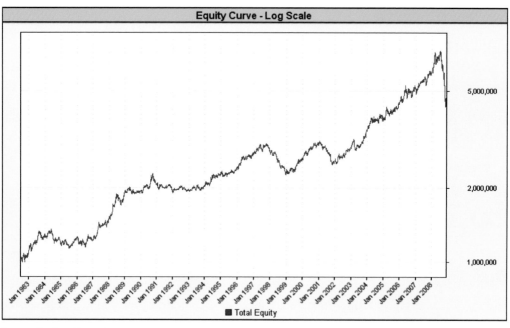

Source: Trading Blox LLC

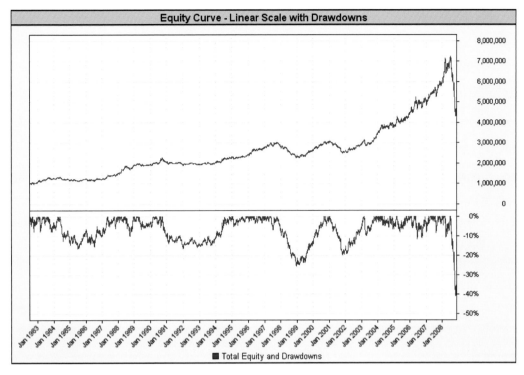

Source: Trading Blox LLC

Additional assumptions

- Any margin arising eliminated by sale of stock

- Re-balance threshold: 5%

- Buffer of 3% deducted from proposed investment amount to account for stock price movement between previous close and next day's open.

Points of note

I do not propose to comment in detail on the less than inspiring statistics arising from the above test. Points of note however are as follows:

Return on collateral

Strip out the return on collateral (I have assumed a fully collateralised investment in Test 5) and the return will look even less exciting.

Cherry picking

I could have produced better back-tested results by cherry picking the portfolio. I could for instance have chosen an energy only portfolio – in contrast to many commodities, oil has had an upward bias over the past 25 years, even after the recent dramatic collapse. But who knows what tomorrow's best performing commodity will be?

Broad diversification

If you take a look at Appendix 1 you will see that instead of cherry picking, I chose to include a wide range of those commodities which are (mostly) available to investors in ETC form, either singly or in combination. As I have touched on before, in my back-testing over the past few years, I have tended to see better results in combining many single markets than in using one index or fund to cover a group of markets. There is more diversification benefit for instance in including gold, silver and platinum separately than in including a single precious metals fund – even if your overall allocation to precious metals remains the same.

Many markets in isolation may look unattractive but may nonetheless add benefit to a portfolio because of a low correlation to other markets within the portfolio. Some markets may not look attractive and in addition do not seem to add to overall profit in a back-test. Nonetheless, I would prefer to include such a market since in the future it may prove to be a winner.

Contango revisited

If you do insist on cherry picking your portfolio (particularly in the commodities sector) be aware that all that glitters is not necessarily gold. I have already explained the elements of return on commodity investment and one of these, you will recall, is roll return. Backwardation makes for a positive roll return and contango for a negative roll return. Contango is typical for a market such as gold, where the futures price takes into account the cost of storage and interest foregone on money tied up. Even if the spot price of a commodity rises over the years, the combination of negative roll yield and an ETC sponsor's fees can mean you end up losing money – even after taking account of the interest on your collateral. You may have seen the spectacular rise of gold this decade. But are you aware what you would have made holding gold in ETC form for the past 26 odd years?

The spot price of gold was $310 an ounce in mid-1982. It was $820 an ounce on 25th November 2008. Call that an annualised return of around 3.75% holding physical gold, before the cost of storage and insurance.

Spot wheat was 341 US cents a bushel in mid-1982 and was 426 cents a bushel on 25th November 2008. On the (fallacious) assumption that you could store physical wheat for that period, that is a miserable annualised return of 0.85% before costs.

Holding gold and wheat via futures

Now take a look what you would have gained holding these commodities through the futures markets on a fully collateralised basis (which is what an ETC does).

Note that the following tests do not include any fees for the ETF sponsor, which would have made a disappointing situation far worse. The effect of negative roll yield has eroded the already meagre benefits to be had from holding these commodities for the period. I hope this may help to explain why a long only holding, even in a diversified basket of commodities, may not offer the sort of rewards an investor may have assumed.

Buy and hold test 7: gold ETC proxy – July 1982 to November 2008

End balance	CAGR%	RAR%	Std dev	Annual Sharpe	Max total equity DD	Longest drawdown	Trades	RSquared
1,650,844	1.92%	0.14%	15.49	-0.07	52.92%	279.2	1	0.18

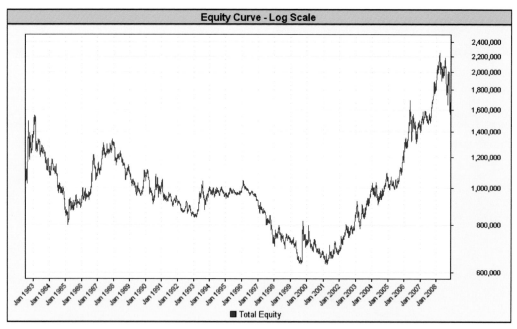

Source: Trading Blox LLC

Source: Trading Blox LLC

Buy and hold test 8: wheat ETC proxy – July 1982 to November 2008

End balance	CAGR%	RAR%	Std dev	Annual Sharpe	Max total equity DD	Longest drawdown	Trades	RSquared
672,591	-1.49	-1.16	22.52	-0.19	85.6%	151	1	4.88

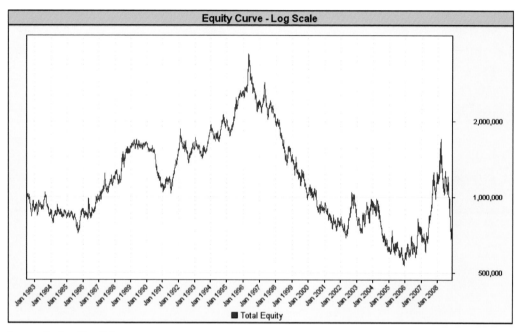

Source: Trading Blox LLC

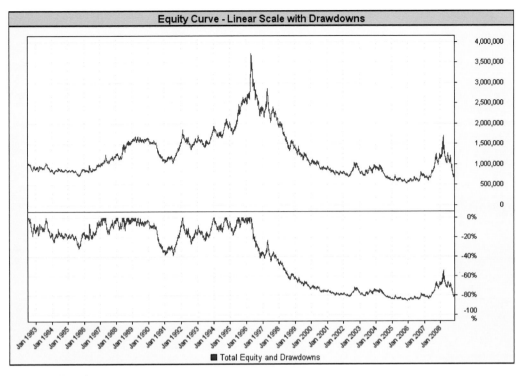

Source: Trading Blox LLC

Further comment

To add insult to injury, look at the maximum drawdown, length of drawdown and risk (in terms of standard deviation) in the above single commodity tests on gold and wheat. On a standalone basis, you would have been far better off keeping your money in the bank. Or rather, in view of recent events, in government bills.

Summary

- **Don't be a sheep**. Freeing yourself from convention and thinking outside of the stifling norms in terms of asset allocation, diversification and weightings can bring substantial benefits.

- **Maximise diversification**. Trading the individual components of a multi-market fund brings greater diversification benefits than trading the multi-market fund itself.

- **Dull but useful**. While making a dull standalone investment, commodities and bills can bring substantial risk reduction to an equities portfolio.

- **Re-balancing**. Re-balancing periodically between stocks, bills and commodities further reduces risk and smoothes the return.

- **Individual commodities**. Holding positions in individual commodities may not produce the returns you might expect. As part of a portfolio however the benefits can be substantial.

What now?

Having established suitable benchmark portfolios and benchmark portfolio returns, we will proceed to better those returns through the use of mechanical, rule-based trading systems.

The Bollinger Band Breakout System

The aims of this chapter are–

- **Description of system.** To describe in detail a simple and effective long-term system to trade Exchange Traded Funds.

- **Performance comparison.** To compare the performance of the system on various portfolios with that of the buy-and-hold benchmark.

- **Diversification.** To explore the benefits or otherwise of adding commodities and short-term debt instruments to a portfolio of equities.

- **Trading short.** To look at the possibility of using the system to benefit from bear markets by taking short trades.

Description of the system

Origins of the system

This system was described by Chuck Le Beau and David Lucas in their book *Technical Traders Guide to Computer Analysis of the Futures Markets*.

What is a Bollinger Band?

A Bollinger Band is a price channel which is defined by placing a band above and below a moving average of price, the band being calculated as one or more standard deviations of the past X day's closing prices, X being the number of days in the moving average. If you find this definition confusing, examples of the system can be seen in the charts further on in this chapter. The standard deviation of past price data is widely used as a measure of volatility and market analyst John Bollinger helped popularise the standard deviation band as a technical indicator.

The purpose of the band

For a trend following system, adding a band or channel around the moving average filters out many of the trades which would otherwise occur when the price whips up and down above and below the moving average, as it tends to do before a firm new upward or downward trend is established.

The moving average

The particular system described in this chapter takes a 200-day simple moving average of the closing price of the relevant instrument and adds further smoothing, averaging the results by 200 days. The latter average is an exponential moving average. The same, so far, as the simple system described in Chapter 1.

Bollinger Band calculation

The Bollinger Band placed above and below the moving average is calculated as one standard deviation of the closing price of the relevant instrument over a period of 200 days.

The rules for long trades

1. Buy at the open the day after the price closes above the upper Bollinger Band.

2. Exit at the open the day after the price closes below the moving average.

The rules for short trades

1. Sell at the open the day after the price closes below the lower Bollinger Band.

2. Exit by buying back when the price closes above the moving average.

The system in long mode

The red line in the chart below represents the 200-day smoothed moving average and the green lines constitute the Bollinger Band envelope which acts to limit whipsaw trades.

Trade entry

The chart depicts the entry of a long trade at the open on 1st September 1982, after the DJI closed above the upper Bollinger Band the previous day.

Trade exit

As can be seen, the trade is exited on 21st February 1984, the DJI having closed below the moving average on the previous day.

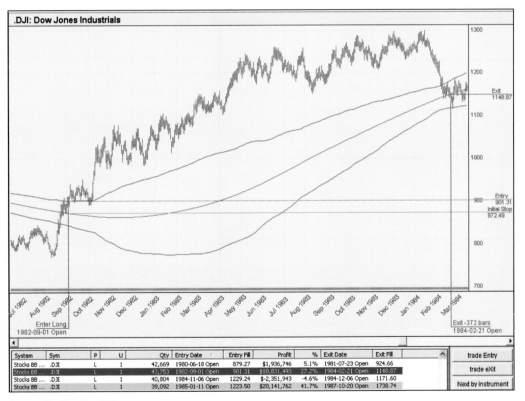

Source: Trading Blox LLC

The system in short mode

The chart below shows a short entry and exit.

Trade entry

The system enters a short trade on 12th November 1973 as the DJI breached the lower Bollinger Band at the close the previous day.

Trade exit

The system exits the short trade on 18th March 1975 as the DJI closed above the moving average at the previous close.

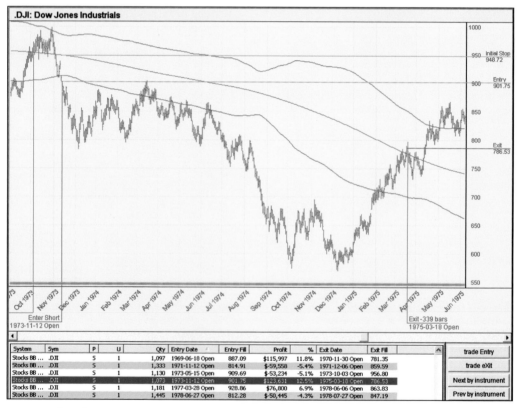

Source: Trading Blox LLC

Illustrating the purpose of the Bollinger Band envelope

The illustrations below show the system, taking both long and short trades, with and without the addition of Bollinger Bands.

Without bands

The chart below shows the simple system described in Chapter 1 and shows the many whipsaw trades which occur as the closing price continually crosses and re-crosses the moving average (the red line).

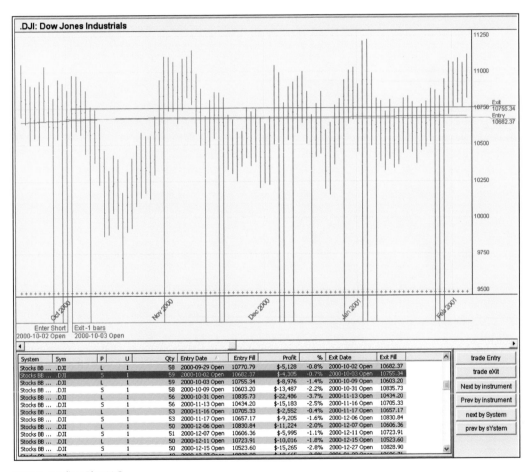

Source: Trading Blox LLC

With bands

The chart below shows the same instrument for the same time period but this time with the addition of the Bollinger Band envelope. As can clearly be seen, the addition of the envelope around the moving average has greatly reduced the number of whipsaw losing trades making for a greatly improved system.

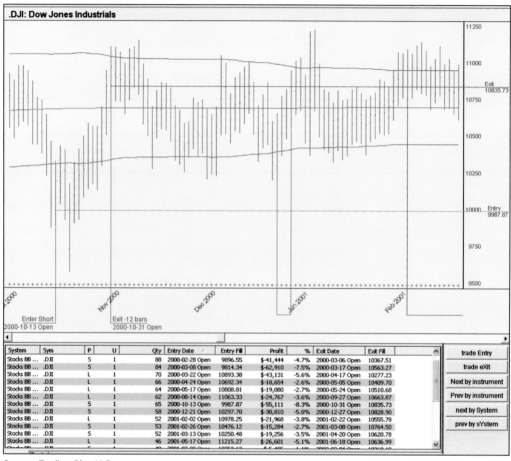

System	Sym	P	U	Qty	Entry Date	Entry Fill	Profit	%	Exit Date	Exit Fill		trade Entry
Stocks BB ...	.DJI	S	1	88	2000-02-28 Open	9896.55	$-41,444	-4.7%	2000-03-06 Open	10367.51		trade eXit
Stocks BB ...	.DJI	S	1	84	2000-03-08 Open	9814.34	$-62,910	-7.5%	2000-03-17 Open	10563.27		
Stocks BB ...	.DJI	L	1	70	2000-03-22 Open	10893.38	$-43,131	-5.6%	2000-04-17 Open	10277.23		Next by instrument
Stocks BB ...	.DJI	L	1	66	2000-04-24 Open	10692.34	$-18,654	-2.6%	2000-05-05 Open	10409.70		
Stocks BB ...	.DJI	L	1	64	2000-05-17 Open	10808.81	$-19,080	-2.7%	2000-05-24 Open	10510.68		Prev by instrument
Stocks BB ...	.DJI	L	1	62	2000-08-14 Open	11063.33	$-24,767	-3.6%	2000-09-27 Open	10663.87		
Stocks BB ...	.DJI	S	1	65	2000-10-13 Open	9987.87	$-55,111	-8.3%	2000-10-31 Open	10835.73		next by System
Stocks BB ...	.DJI	S	1	58	2000-12-21 Open	10297.70	$-30,810	-5.0%	2000-12-27 Open	10828.90		prev by sYstem
Stocks BB ...	.DJI	L	1	52	2001-02-02 Open	10978.25	$-21,968	-3.8%	2001-02-22 Open	10555.78		
Stocks BB ...	.DJI	S	1	53	2001-02-26 Open	10476.12	$-15,284	-2.7%	2001-03-08 Open	10764.50		
Stocks BB ...	.DJI	S	1	52	2001-03-13 Open	10250.48	$-19,256	-3.5%	2001-04-20 Open	10620.78		
Stocks BB ...	.DJI	L	1	46	2001-05-17 Open	11215.27	$-26,601	-5.1%	2001-06-18 Open	10636.99		

Source: Trading Blox LLC

Money management and test assumptions

The basic money management technique I have adopted in the tests in this chapter is to divide the total account equity equally between the number of indices/ETF proxies in the portfolio for which I have price data available on the given date.

Set out below you will find a screen shot of the Trading Blox Graphical User Interface for this system, which may help to illustrate the assumptions used in the tests in this chapter.

Global Parameters	Stocks BB Breakout	
System: Stocks BB Breakout		
Portfolio Manager		▲
○ Futures		
● Stocks	Dividend Stocks	▼
○ Forex		
Trade Direction (Long/Short/All)	Trade Long	▼
Minimum MM Signals	Step ☐	1
Entries and Exits		▲
Rebalance Threshold	Step ☐	5%
Rebalance Frequency	Quarterly	▼
Eliminate Margin	True	▼
MM Equity	Trading Equity	▼
Percentage Commission	Step ☐	0.3%
Leverage	Step ☐	1
MM Algorithm	Trading Instruments	▼
Buffer	Step ☐	3%
Close Average (bars)	Step ☐	200
Entry Threshold (std dev)	Step ☐	2
Exit Threshold (std dev)	Step ☐	0
Exits	On Open	▼
Risk Manager		▲
Auxiliary		▲
Monthly Incentive (%)	Step ☐	0%
Net Assets (%)	Step ☐	1.5%
Charge Fees	True	▼

Source: Trading Blox LLC

Points to note

MM algorithm

This is set to "Trading Instruments" – both words are of my own choosing and merely signify the money management algorithm devised and used in this system and in the tests in this chapter. I have defined "Trading Instruments" in code to equal the number of instruments in a portfolio for which I have trading data at a given date. Assume that it is the end of December 2003; at that time, all 26 instruments in Portfolio 1 are "trading" – therefore "Trading Instruments" equates to 26 at that date.

Example

Assume that the start date used in a test is towards the end of December 2003 and that start up capital is USD1m. The money management algorithm divides USD1m by 26 giving $38,462. At that time, 16 indices traded above the relevant 200-day moving average and so (ignoring costs) $38,462 will be invested in each such index. Approximately 60% of the account will be invested ($615,392) while the 40% balance (384,608) remains in cash or bills. The same procedure is used for re-balancing: positions valued at over 1/26th of the account value in December 2003 would be sold down and positions valued at less than 1/26th would be increased.

Re-balance threshold

This, set at 5%, means that unless a position is out of kilter by more than 5%, no re-balancing of that position will take place. This saves a lot of expense and a great number of marginal trades.

Buffer

Again, a word of my own choosing, to represent a particular parameter and segment of coding. Position size (the number of shares to be bought or sold) is based on the latest closing price for the relevant market. Markets often open at a different level to the previous close on which the calculations were based – you may end up paying more for your stock or receiving less than you had expected. The coding behind "Buffer" therefore reduces the amount of a stock purchased (whether on an initial purchase or as part of a re-balancing exercise) by the specified percentage (3% in these tests) and increases the amount of a stock sale (on re-balancing only) by the same percentage. This helps to ensure that margin is not unintentionally incurred and that a cash float is kept in the account.

Eliminate margin

When this parameter is set to "True", any margin which arises in the account will be dealt with the following day when stocks are sold down proportionately to eliminate the deficit.

Minimum MM signals

This parameter can be used to ensure that capital is not invested in too narrow a range of stocks. The number of "Trading Instruments" builds up to 26 by late 2003 but there are times when "Trading Instruments" number far less than this figure. If the number of

Trading Instruments at the relevant time is less than the figure chosen for "Minimum MM Signals", then for position sizing purposes the account equity will be divided by the greater number. I have used a setting of 1 for the tests in this chapter thus account equity has simply been divided by the number of "Trading Instruments" at a given date.

MM equity

For all tests in this book I have assumed that the equity to be used is the full marked-to-market account value.

Leverage

I have assumed no leverage for the tests in this book.

Percentage commission

Where brokerage commission has been used in these tests I have set it at 0.3% of the total dollar or relevant currency amount of the trade.

Net assets (%), charge fees

Where stated, I have assumed an annual charge of 1.5% of the net assets in the account (0.125% debited each month). This is on top of commissions and goes some way towards simulating management fees, expenses and tracking error in a widely diversified portfolio of index tracking ETFs.

Global parameters

This tab gives the user many other test parameter choices such as slippage levels, restrictions on trading more than a certain percentage of the average daily volume and the ability to run stepped start dates in a single test.

Code available for download

I have posted this system (coded for Trading Blox) under the heading "Blox Market Place" on the Trading Blox Forum. For as long as the proprietor cares to keep the forum open and my post in existence, users of Trading Blox can download the system for free.

Performance comparison: the Dow with and without the Bollinger Band envelope

It would be useful to ascertain how the Bollinger Band System fares in a back-test on the Dow and compare it to the back-tests of both the simple moving average system and buy-and-hold in Chapter 1. Set out below, you will see the answer. I have used exactly the same assumptions as were used in the earlier test.

Bollinger Band breakout test 1: the Dow 1st January 1900 to 4th November 2008, long only

End balance	CAGR%	RAR%	Std dev	Annual Sharpe	Max total equity DD	Longest drawdown	Trades	RSquared
209,894,808	5.03%	5.11%	11.66	0.14	39.7%	204.6	77	97.07

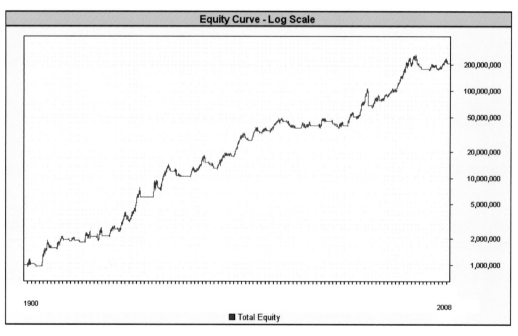

Source: Trading Blox LLC

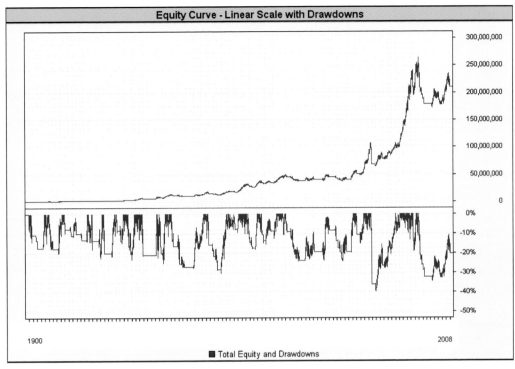

Source: Trading Blox LLC

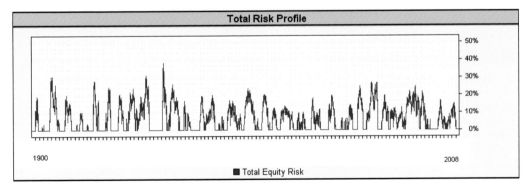

Source: Trading Blox LLC

Assumptions

- Starting capital USD1m.
- Base currency is US dollars.
- Risk Free Rate is 3%.
- Income does not accrue on any un-invested balances.
- Price only index used – cash dividends are not included.
- No slippage, commission, or Total Expense Ratio is assumed.

Comparison table

For ease of comparison, I set out a table of relevant figures below:

	Bollinger Band Breakout	Simple System	Buy and Hold
CAGR	5.03%	5.19%	4.65%
Risk adjusted CAGR	5.03%	4.95%	2.92%
RAR	5.11%	5.55%	5.0%
Risk adjusted RAR	5.11%	5.29%	3.14%
Max total equity drawdown	39.7%	50.8%	89.20%
Average max drawdown	31.48%	37.4%	55.09%
Longest drawdown	204.6 months	105.8 months	302.8 months
Average max drawdown length	111	86.22 months	142.14 months
Standard deviation	11.66	12.22	18.57
Winning months	954	903	750
Losing months	353	404	557
Winning trades	32 (41.6%)	50 (16.9%)	1 (100%)
Losing trades	45 (58.4%)	245 (83.1%)	0

At first glance, the difference may not appear that startling but on closer inspection it can be seen to offer significant advantages (as explained below).

CAGR/RAR

On a risk adjusted basis, the new system with Bollinger Bands only just outperforms the simple system: a CAGR of 5.03% for the former as opposed to risk adjusted 4.95% for the latter (note the slightly higher standard deviation of the simpler system). RAR is slightly higher for the simple system even after adjusting for risk.

Drawdown

Both maximum drawdown and average maximum drawdown have been significantly reduced by the addition of Bollinger Bands, making the system less hair-raising to trade. Unfortunately, in this test, the Bollinger Band System records much longer drawdowns.

Number of trades

As expected, the number of trades has been greatly reduced by the addition of bands: from 295 to 77. This makes for a system which is a lot easier to trade, as well as less prone to slippage, opening gaps and drag from commission. If your estimates for slippage and commission turn out to be optimistic, that will have far less effect on a system which trades less often. Look at the proportion of winning to losing trades: the new system (where winning trades are 41% of the total) is going to be far easier to trade in psychological terms than a system where only 16.9% of trades are profitable.

Total risk profile

I have introduced a new Trading Blox chart here: "Total Risk Profile". Risk is defined as the distance from the close to the stop price on any given day and since this is a system without stops as such, the moving average is used as an approximation.

The system had zero risk for around 42% of this entire 108 year period: the system was out of the market for periods totalling approximately 46 years. For those periods where the system was in the market, the average system risk was 11% and maximum risk just under 40%. So, leaving aside the question of whether you could or would actually have been able to exit at the moving average, for much of the period only 11% of your capital was at risk. With buy and hold, your risk is 100% of your capital at all times.

The advantage of spending long periods of time out of the market, when conditions are not propitious, (in interest-earning cash or short-term bonds), is obvious. It also acts to greatly decrease the volatility (standard deviation) of your investment. This, if you like, is part of the fabled *money management* concept – having stops (or at least defined exit points) to limit your risk.

Performance comparison with buy and hold on equal weighted equity indices

In an earlier chapter I demonstrated that buying and holding an equally weighted portfolio of international equity indices, or a weighting system other than market capitalisation, may provide greater diversification than holding one diversified index such as the MSCI World, and at least the chance of better returns.

Too much dependence on a given market will be beneficial when that market outperforms but will be a drag on performance at other times. An investor has much more flexibility than a big institution to give more weight to smaller markets than is justified by market capitalisation, and need not feel obliged to give a 50% allocation in his portfolio to the US or a 10% allocation to the UK.

Set out below you will see how the Bollinger Band Breakout System performs on Portfolio 1.

Bollinger Band breakout test 2: portfolio 1, 1st January 1980 to 20th November 2008, long only

End balance	CAGR %	RAR %	Std dev	Annual Sharpe	Max total equity DD	Longest drawdown	Trades	RSquared
45,576,553	14.12	13.99	10.64	0.86	24.0%	44.2	942	95.59

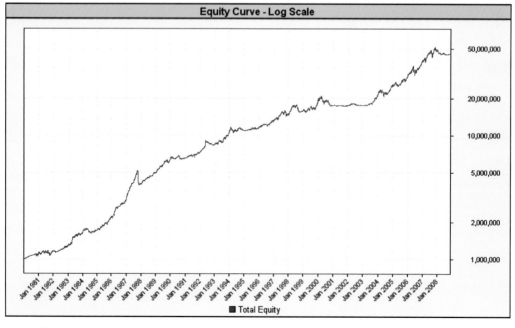

Source: Trading Blox LLC

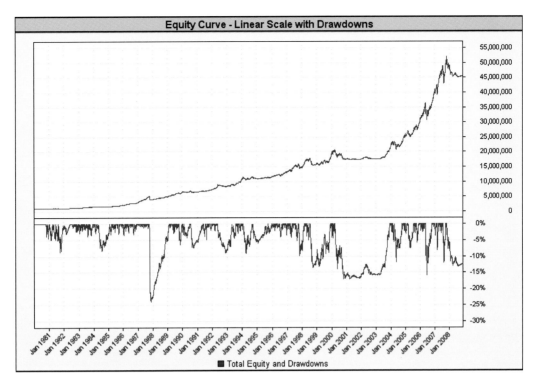

Source: Trading Blox LLC

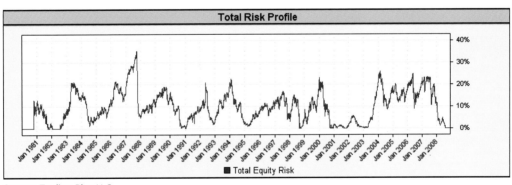

Source: Trading Blox LLC

Assumptions

Parameter	Value
Starting capital	USD1m
Base currency	US dollars
Risk free rate	3%
Interest	At the rate of three-month US Government T Bills accrues on un-invested balances
Dividends	Price only indices used but cash dividends are collected and re-invested quarterly
Re-balancing	Quarterly
Margin	Any arising eliminated by sale of stock
Re-balance threshold	5%
Buffer	3% deducted from investment amount to account for stock price movement between previous close and next day's open
Slippage	10%
Commission	0.3% of the dollar value of the transaction
Annual Total Expense Ratio (TER)	1.5% is assumed (in addition to commissions) to simulate the effect of management fees and all other costs of an ETF

Comparison table

For ease of comparison, I set out a table of relevant figures below:

	Bollinger Band Breakout	Buy and Hold	Buy and Hold adjusted for risk
CAGR	14.12%	12.7%	7.99%
RAR	13.99%	15.86%	9.98%
Max total equity drawdown	24%	58.9%	
Average max drawdown	16.68%	38.54%	
Longest drawdown	44.2 months	45.9 months	
Average max drawdown length	22.17 months	38.54 months	
Standard deviation	10.64	16.91	
Winning months	252 (72.6%)	226 (65%)	
Losing months	95 (27.4%)	121 (35%)	

Points to note

CAGR/RAR

As can be seen, on a risk adjusted basis the Bollinger Band Breakout system greatly outperformed buy-and-hold.

Maximum drawdown

In November 2008, the buy-and-hold investor was sitting on a 58.9% loss in the value of his account following the high of October 2007. The user of the Bollinger Band Breakout System began to exit his positions in early November 2007; by the end of January 2008 he was out of over 70% of his equity positions and sitting in cash or bills. The last positions for the BBBO investor were disposed of in July 2008, as the commodity and raw material related stock markets, such as Canada and Russia, met their exit signals in line with the savage downturn in oil, metals, grains and almost every other physical commodity. The BBBO System ended the period with a drawdown from its October 2007 equity peak of a mere 12.25%.

Average maximum drawdown length

While the longest drawdown figures are roughly equal, the system records on average a maximum drawdown length roughly half that of buy-and-hold. This reflects both lower magnitude of drawdowns in the first place and quicker recovery thanks to interest earned on cash while un-invested.

Winning months

Notice the greater percentage of winning months using the Bollinger Breakout System: sitting in interest earning cash during the bad times increases the number of months where a positive performance is achieved.

Standard deviation

With long periods out of the market and well timed exits, the volatility or risk of this portfolio traded with the Bollinger Band System is 37% less than when it is simply bought and held.

Caveat

It is important not to misinterpret these results, which were arrived at by using one set of parameters of one system, one portfolio and one time period. You will get very different figures once you start altering the parameters, portfolios and assumptions from those that I have used.

What is likely to remain however, is a common thread: on balance, using a simple mechanical system such as this will usually have you out of the market before the worst happens and will have you back in when a clear upward trend once again becomes apparent.

Stepping the start and end dates

Considerable differences in CAGR result from adjusting start and end dates and it is useful to run tests over different time periods to see the effect it has on return, drawdown and other factors.

To illustrate the point, I set out below stepped parameter test results for buy-and-hold and the BBBO system using exactly the same portfolio and settings as I used in Test 2 above.

The results show 20 different 10-year periods, each 10-year period commencing and ending on the date given in the table below.

Test 3: buy and hold stepped start date parameter test

Source: Trading Blox LLC

Start	End	Ending balance	CAGR%	MAR	Annual Sharpe	Max total equity DD	Longest drawdown	Trades	Rsquared
01/01/1980	29/12/1989	7,415,764.64	22.18%	0.7	0.97	31.50%	22.2	338	87.34
31/12/1980	29/12/1990	5,290,489.17	18.13%	0.58	0.7	31.30%	22.2	398	91.81
31/12/1981	29/12/1991	6,432,044.84	20.46%	0.66	0.85	31.10%	14.9	444	95.67
31/12/1982	28/12/1992	8,294,094.53	23.56%	0.76	1.17	31.10%	13.8	501	95.02
31/12/1983	28/12/1993	8,829,764.41	24.34%	0.78	1.19	31.10%	13.8	514	93.97
30/12/1984	28/12/1994	8,817,121.33	24.32%	0.78	1.17	31.10%	13.2	534	93.17
30/12/1985	28/12/1995	7,299,112.31	21.99%	0.71	1.03	31.10%	13.2	536	93.66
30/12/1986	27/12/1996	6,084,722.36	19.79%	0.64	0.98	31.00%	13.1	551	96.56
30/12/1987	27/12/1997	4,408,202.90	15.99%	0.81	0.82	19.70%	13.1	539	97.69
29/12/1988	27/12/1998	3,651,759.09	13.83%	0.49	0.8	28.20%	13.2	541	96.72
29/12/1989	27/12/1999	3,844,778.32	14.42%	0.51	0.77	28.30%	13.2	550	96.67
29/12/1990	26/12/2000	3,550,571.67	13.51%	0.48	0.61	28.30%	12	541	96.41
29/12/1991	26/12/2001	2,617,391.75	10.10%	0.25	0.39	41.10%	21	592	89.88
28/12/1992	26/12/2002	2,122,513.75	7.82%	0.18	0.25	43.00%	33	551	76.25
28/12/1993	26/12/2003	2,156,490.69	7.99%	0.19	0.26	42.80%	45	502	63.25
28/12/1994	25/12/2004	2,577,737.91	9.93%	0.23	0.34	42.90%	46.1	507	63.6
28/12/1995	25/12/2005	2,871,340.36	11.12%	0.26	0.4	43.00%	46.1	538	64.2
27/12/1996	25/12/2006	3,327,223.40	12.77%	0.3	0.45	43.20%	46.6	512	65.23
27/12/1997	25/12/2007	3,868,256.10	14.48%	0.34	0.53	42.10%	45.9	480	71.3
27/12/1998	20/11/2008	1,522,476.83	4.33%	0.07	0.05	58.20%	45.9	470	72.27

Bollinger Band breakout test 4: Bollinger Band breakout stepped start date parameter test

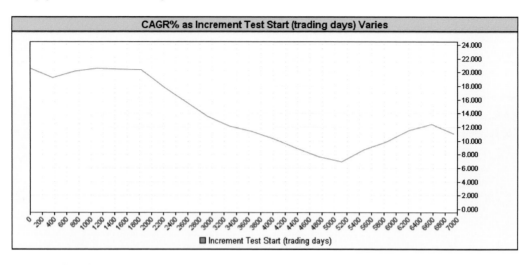

Source: Trading Blox LLC

Start	End	Ending balance	CAGR%	MAR	Annual Sharpe	Max total equity	Longest DD	Trades	Rsq	Win duration	Loss duration
01/01/1980	29/12/1989	6,497,608.01	20.58%	0.86	1.41	24.00%	16.1	203	94.83	464.3	107.73
31/12/1980	29/12/1990	5,805,975.70	19.23%	0.8	1.11	24.00%	16.1	219	96.84	471.64	114.88
31/12/1981	29/12/1991	6,282,561.95	20.18%	0.84	1.23	24.00%	16.1	244	96.86	460.93	107.51
31/12/1982	28/12/1992	6,505,358.94	20.59%	0.86	1.28	24.00%	16.1	281	95.98	443.4	103.48
31/12/1983	28/12/1993	6,431,356.98	20.46%	0.85	1.28	24.00%	16.1	313	94.56	401.34	102.21
30/12/1984	28/12/1994	6,399,851.11	20.40%	0.85	1.26	24.00%	16.1	327	93.85	406.34	100.06
30/12/1985	28/12/1995	5,209,980.13	17.95%	0.75	1.07	24.00%	19.6	340	94.22	363.31	91.98
30/12/1986	27/12/1996	4,313,392.30	15.74%	0.66	1.04	24.00%	22.7	341	96.62	362.93	98.35
30/12/1987	27/12/1997	3,573,472.60	13.58%	1.38	0.99	9.90%	22.7	347	97.41	400.09	102.34
29/12/1988	27/12/1998	3,146,778.90	12.15%	0.9	0.91	13.60%	22.7	363	97.72	451	100.26
29/12/1989	27/12/1999	2,933,916.06	11.36%	0.83	0.96	13.60%	22.9	393	97.1	422.51	94.63
29/12/1990	26/12/2000	2,658,507.01	10.27%	0.61	0.66	16.90%	22.9	418	96.47	426.25	101.58
29/12/1991	26/12/2001	2,349,888.11	8.92%	0.53	0.53	17.00%	22.9	396	92.97	425.1	103.83
28/12/1992	26/12/2002	2,095,755.49	7.68%	0.45	0.41	17.00%	33	377	88	426.11	105.67
28/12/1993	26/12/2003	1,958,164.12	6.95%	0.41	0.39	16.80%	44.2	373	83.37	394.52	112.63
28/12/1994	25/12/2004	2,305,906.03	8.71%	0.52	0.53	16.80%	44.2	351	83.29	438.2	105.67
28/12/1995	25/12/2005	2,565,044.58	9.88%	0.59	0.62	16.80%	44.2	364	82.51	448.39	115.38
27/12/1996	25/12/2006	2,976,239.27	11.52%	0.68	0.67	16.80%	44.2	376	78.66	437.38	109.23
27/12/1997	25/12/2007	3,224,387.38	12.42%	0.73	0.7	17.00%	44.4	378	78.6	472.82	101.38
27/12/1998	20/11/2008	2,825,600.09	11.04%	0.65	0.54	17.10%	44.4	343	84.92	532.72	102.65

Points to note

Decelerating performance

Most obvious from the graph is the decelerating performance of the equity markets over the period. After a period of very high growth in world equity markets in the 1980s and 1990s, the past decade has been less kind.

Robust

On these tests at least and using this portfolio, the BBBO system has shown itself robust to changes in start and end dates. The CAGR is often lower for a given period than for buy-and-hold, but the BBBO system makes up lost ground during a severe drawdown and consistently reduces the maximum drawdown.

MAR

Note the consistently higher MAR and Annual Sharpe ratios for the BBBO system over those of buy-and-hold: equivalent gain for much less pain and far less volatility. Put at its simplest, the use of such a system is a far more comfortable way to invest.

Win/loss duration

Note the columns "Win Duration" and "Loss Duration" in Test 4. These reflect, for each test period, the average length in calendar days for winning and losing trades. Note that, as is essential for a successful trend following system, winners are allowed to run, while losers are swiftly stopped out. As can be seen, in this test winners tend to average a holding period of 12 to 18 months, while losers last only around 3 months.

There is a lot of nonsense talked about market timing, and journalists in particular are fond of quoting the old saw about how being absent from the markets for such and such a period would have destroyed an investor's return. One can only assume that those who talk along such lines have never actually taken the trouble to investigate mechanical systems.

Stepping the moving average length and the standard deviation bands

Optimisation

So far, we have only considered a moving average length of 200 days and an envelope of one standard deviation of the closing price over a 200-day period. It is important to investigate how robust these parameters are and whether better parameters or a group of better parameters can be found. It is also important to see how performance varies over time: a 100 day moving average in conjunction with a 0.5 standard deviation envelope may have produced better results in the 1980s, but what looks to be the optimal system for the 1990s and the current decade?

Has the situation changed?

Time periods

I take 3 different periods:

- 1st January 1980 to 29th December 1989;

- 29th December 1989 to 27th December 1999; and

- 27th December 1999 to 20th November 2008.

Parameter stepping

For each period I step the moving average from 100 to 400 days in increments of 100. For each of these 4 different moving average lengths, I test 4 different band widths from 0.5 Std Dev to 2 Std Dev in increments of 0.5 Std Dev. The result is 48 different tests. If too many parameters are stepped at the same time, the number of tests becomes unwieldy and the results may be difficult to interpret. In a more complex system, it would be better to adopt a "hunt and peck" process, testing a limited number of variables at any one time and then gradually honing in on the optimal areas for further investigation. Again, I used exactly the same portfolio and test settings as used in Bollinger Band Breakout Test 2 above.

Bollinger Band breakout test 5: stepping the moving average and std dev bands

Period: 1st January 1980 to 29th December 1989

MA days	Entry band std dev	Ending balance	CAGR (%)	Annual Sharpe	Max total DD	Longest DD	Trades	Std dev	Win duration (days)	Loss duration (days)
100	0.5	6,975,598.97	21.44%	1.46	21.00%	16.1	280	11.18	272	42
100	1	6,629,517.74	20.82%	1.49	21.00%	17.3	254	11.09	277	46
100	1.5	6,644,225.07	20.85%	1.54	21.00%	18.2	228	10.86	286	51
100	2	6,057,006.23	19.73%	1.39	20.40%	18.2	221	10.64	280	62
200	0.5	6,247,496.20	20.11%	1.37	25.60%	17.2	239	11.99	438	78
200	1	6,497,608.01	20.58%	1.41	24.00%	16.1	203	11.67	464	108
200	1.5	6,329,678.07	20.27%	1.33	21.40%	15.7	185	11.22	456	115
200	2	5,867,968.93	19.36%	1.32	21.40%	16.1	175	10.97	454	98
300	0.5	6,160,829.76	19.94%	1.21	23.80%	15.8	212	12.1	499	104
300	1	5,904,363.65	19.43%	1.14	23.80%	16.7	192	12	516	122
300	1.5	5,676,275.73	18.96%	1.1	23.80%	18.1	176	11.72	522	136
300	2	6,063,896.92	19.75%	1.36	23.80%	16.2	164	11.28	518	177
400	0.5	6,089,355.72	19.80%	1.21	27.60%	17.3	210	13.05	507	126
400	1	6,362,704.80	20.33%	1.33	26.00%	16.6	189	12.47	524	163
400	1.5	5,957,865.10	19.54%	1.34	26.10%	16.7	180	12.23	517	166
400	2	5,769,845.73	19.16%	1.29	26.10%	17.1	164	12.1	542	159

Period: 29th December 1989 to 27th December 1999

MA days	Entry band std dev	Ending balance	CAGR (%)	Annual Sharpe	Max total DD	Longest DD	Trades	Std dev	Win duration (days)	Loss duration (days)
100	0.5	3,282,790.15	12.62%	0.9	11.20%	26.4	601	10.16	238	46
100	1	3,139,441.01	12.12%	0.94	9.40%	25.5	508	9.82	249	62
100	1.5	2,994,691.79	11.59%	0.92	8.90%	25.5	456	9.54	255	72
100	2	2,962,507.79	11.47%	1.01	8.90%	25.6	408	9.1	251	75
200	0.5	3,080,564.59	11.91%	0.94	13.60%	12.1	436	10.15	417	78
200	1	2,933,916.06	11.36%	0.96	13.60%	22.9	393	10.01	423	95
200	1.5	2,852,418.70	11.05%	1.04	13.50%	17.8	350	9.65	425	109
200	2	2,860,068.94	11.08%	1.13	13.40%	19.4	298	9.31	426	115
300	0.5	2,842,464.59	11.01%	0.84	16.60%	19.1	426	10.35	502	95
300	1	2,782,022.95	10.77%	0.88	16.30%	17.4	373	10.1	524	123
300	1.5	2,685,540.35	10.38%	0.9	16.00%	16.5	335	9.73	538	130
300	2	2,670,408.94	10.32%	0.97	15.90%	16.6	301	9.4	527	129
400	0.5	2,480,108.08	9.51%	0.69	18.90%	21	404	10.1	655	119
400	1	2,596,227.57	10.01%	0.78	18.20%	15.9	342	9.83	670	177
400	1.5	2,530,420.45	9.73%	0.8	18.10%	15.9	321	9.57	674	199
400	2	2,449,435.30	9.37%	0.82	18.20%	16.8	286	9.27	673	214

Period: 27th December 1999 to 20th November 2008

MA days	Entry band std dev	Ending balance	CAGR (%)	Annual Sharpe	Max total DD	Longest DD	Trades	Std dev	Win duration (days)	Loss duration (days)
100	0.5	2,185,913.41	9.17%	0.45	18.40%	42.4	511	9.34	269	37
100	1	2,204,541.02	9.27%	0.47	16.60%	42.4	402	9.1	271	57
100	1.5	2,159,382.98	9.02%	0.49	14.30%	42.3	340	8.86	291	71
100	2	2,047,167.51	8.37%	0.48	13.20%	42.4	306	8.4	288	75
200	0.5	2,373,934.49	10.18%	0.46	18.00%	44.2	344	9.7	549	87
200	1	2,326,900.61	9.93%	0.47	16.90%	44.3	292	9.47	573	115
200	1.5	2,258,361.99	9.57%	0.46	16.90%	45.1	248	9.17	599	133
200	2	2,171,820.79	9.09%	0.44	16.30%	45.4	232	8.9	621	149
300	0.5	2,075,372.26	8.53%	0.34	22.50%	55.1	315	10.23	668	137
300	1	2,112,364.60	8.75%	0.37	20.60%	55.1	276	10	690	181
300	1.5	2,037,968.03	8.31%	0.35	19.80%	55.4	265	9.81	705	181
300	2	1,903,756.84	7.49%	0.3	19.00%	56.1	234	9.6	669	190
400	0.5	1,800,372.89	6.82%	0.23	25.30%	57.1	313	10.72	716	166
400	1	1,797,527.78	6.80%	0.23	24.30%	57.1	276	10.39	734	209
400	1.5	1,750,865.45	6.48%	0.22	22.40%	58.7	244	10.29	724	236
400	2	1,661,348.71	5.86%	0.18	22.40%	63.8	234	10.03	730	237

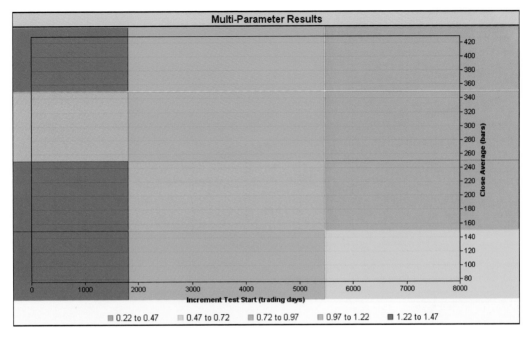

Source: Trading Blox LLC

Comment

The above graph (optimised to illustrate the Sharpe Ratio) helps to illustrate that the highest (best) annual Sharpe Ratio was attained at the beginning of the period and deteriorated throughout, as returns declined while the annualised standard deviation of returns (or volatility/risk) remained more constant. Note that in the middle period, the best Sharpe Ratio was obtained by Moving Averages in the 200-day range, while in the most recent period, the highest scores were made by Moving Averages in the 100 to 200-day range.

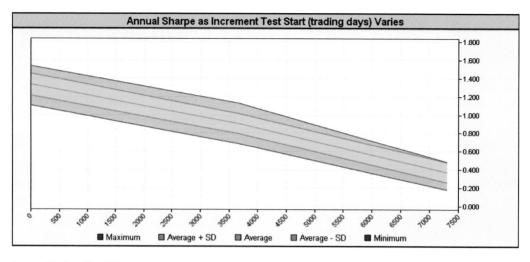

Source: Trading Blox LLC

Comment

Again, note from the above chart that the Sharpe Ratio has declined over the period as returns have deteriorated and risk has remained more or less constant.

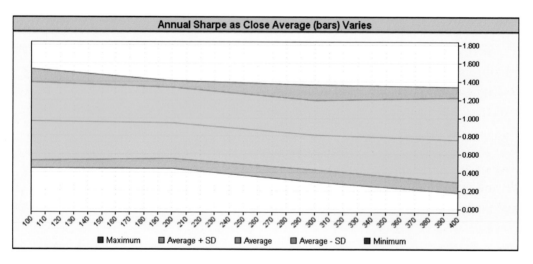

Source: Trading Blox LLC

Comment

As can be seen from the above chart, the best Sharpe Ratios are obtained from the shorter moving averages and the 200-day moving average looks to be a reasonable choice, since the Sharpe Ratio drops off as the moving average days increase to the right of the chart.

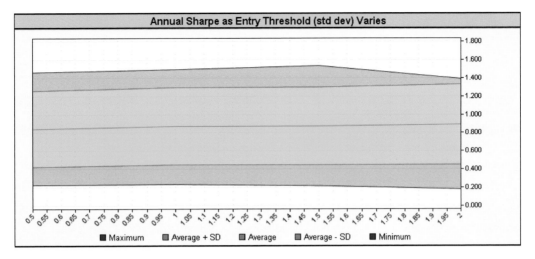

Source: Trading Blox LLC

Comment

As regards the multiple of Standard Deviation of closing price used to form the Bollinger Bands, note that one standard deviation seems a reasonable choice to use in conjunction with any of the moving averages in any of the three time periods.

All combinations profitable

Note, in more general terms, that every combination of moving average and standard deviation band in every time period was profitable.

Fast / slow systems

The faster the moving average (the lower the number of days used in its calculation) and the lower the multiple of standard deviations used for the bands, the "faster" the system and the less time spent in a trade. Faster systems enter quicker, exit sooner and generate more trades than slower systems. While faster systems seemed the clear winners in the first period of the test, the middle parameters seemed to have won the day by the final test period.

Keep parameters under review

200 days and one standard deviation look a reasonable choice for the present but clearly the next ten years may present a further shift in optimal parameters.

Adding commodities and short-term bills

Does the addition of commodities and short-term debt instruments to the portfolio bring benefits?

Portfolio allocation

I conducted the same experiment in Chapter 5 on a buy-and-hold basis and now look to see how the Bollinger Band Breakout system benefits from the same asset allocation. In this test a 20% weighting is given to 3-month US Government Treasury Bills, 20% to commodities (Portfolio 2, Appendix 1) and 60% to equities (Portfolio 1, Appendix 1).

Re-balancing

Re-balancing is undertaken quarterly and takes two forms:

1. **Between asset classes.** As between asset classes, each quarter bills, commodities and equities are re-balanced to maintain the 20/20/60 split.

2. **Within asset classes.** Within the commodities allocation, each commodity is re-balanced each quarter so as to maintain equal exposure to each commodity within the commodities portfolio which is trading above its 200-day moving average. Within the equities allocation, each country index is re-balanced each quarter to maintain equal exposure to each index in Portfolio 1, which is trading above its 200-day moving average.

Parameters

We revert to a moving average of 200 days and a standard deviation band of one.

Bollinger Band breakout test 6: equities, commodities, bills 1st January 1980 to 20th November 2008

End balance	CAGR %	RAR %	Std dev	Annual Sharpe	Max total equity DD	Longest drawdown	Trades	RSquared
21,874,395	11.26	10.87	6.75	1	14.5	42.2	2319	96.23

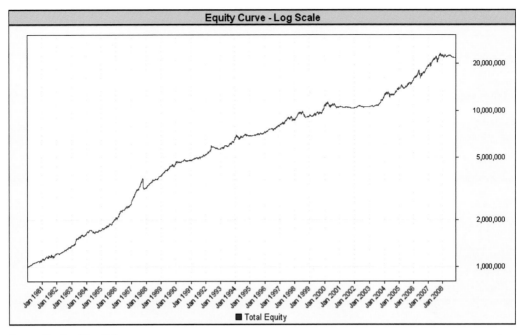

Source: Trading Blox LLC

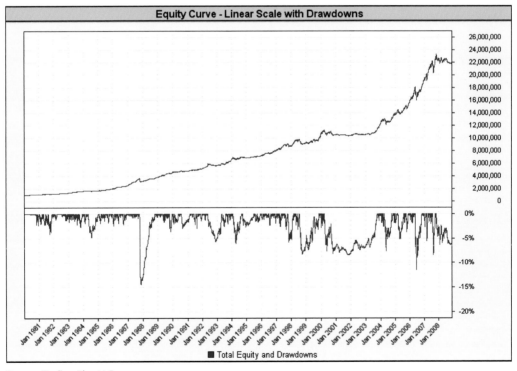

Source: Trading Blox LLC

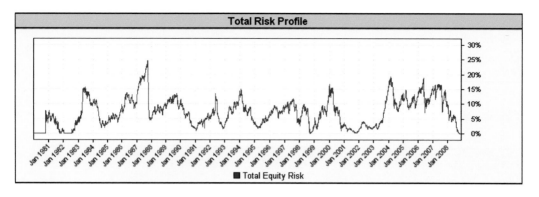

Source: Trading Blox LLC

Assumptions

Parameter	Value
Starting capital	USD1m
Base currency	US dollars
Risk free rate	3%
Interest	Three-month US Government T-Bills accrues on un-invested balances
Dividends	Price only indices used for equities but cash dividends are collected and re-invested quarterly
Yield	Commodity indices include roll yield and collateral yield
Re-balancing	Quarterly
Margin	Any arising eliminated by sale of stock
Re-balance threshold	5%
Buffer	3%
Slippage	10%
Commission	0.3% of the dollar value of the transaction
Annual fees	1.5% assumed

Comparison table

I set out below a table to compare the effects of using the system to trade equities only (Bollinger Band Breakout Test 2) and the asset allocation tested above (Bollinger Band Breakout Test 6):

Bollinger Band Breakout	Equities Only	Stocks/Bills/Commodities
CAGR	14.12%	11.26%
Risk adjusted CAGR	8.96%	11.26%
RAR	13.99%	10.87%
Risk adjusted RAR	8.87%	10.87%
Max total equity drawdown	24%	14.5%
Average max drawdown	16.68%	10.23%
Longest drawdown	44.2 months	42.2 months
Average max drawdown length	22.17 months	38.54 months
Standard deviation	10.64	6.75
Winning months	252 (72.6%)	256 (73.8%)
Losing months	95 (27.4%)	91 (26.2%)
Winning trades	562 (73.6%)	1475 (63.6%)
Losing trades	202 (26.4%)	844 (36.4%)

Points to note

Adding commodities and short-term bills has reaped considerable benefits:

CAGR/RAR

Although the absolute returns of an equities only investment are considerably higher, the price is much higher volatility. When adjusting these returns for the much lower volatility of the more diversified portfolio, it can be seen that the logical investor would choose the latter.

Drawdown

Maximum total equity drawdown and average maximum drawdown have been cut by around 40% by the addition of bills and commodities, while absolute CAGR has been diminished by only 20%.

Choice

It boils down to a simple choice: do you want to accept more risk and volatility in return for higher absolute rewards? Or do you want a much smoother ride and lower absolute returns?

Commodities only

For the sake of completeness, the test results set out below show the operation of the system with identical parameters and assumptions on Commodities only – Portfolio 2.

Bollinger Band breakout test 7: commodities only, 1st January 1980 to 20th November 2008

End balance	CAGR %	RAR %	Std dev	Annual Sharpe	Max total equity DD	Longest drawdown	Trades	RSquared
6,995,906	7.64	7.09	7.12	0.68	18.3	33.3	1214	97.45

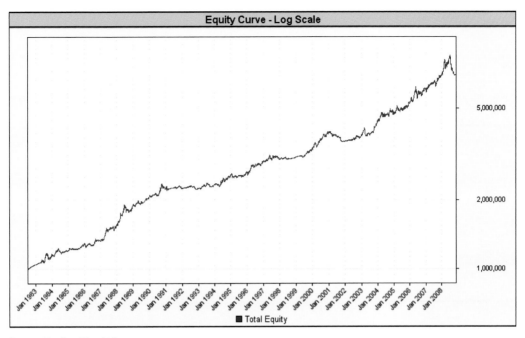

Source: Trading Blox LLC

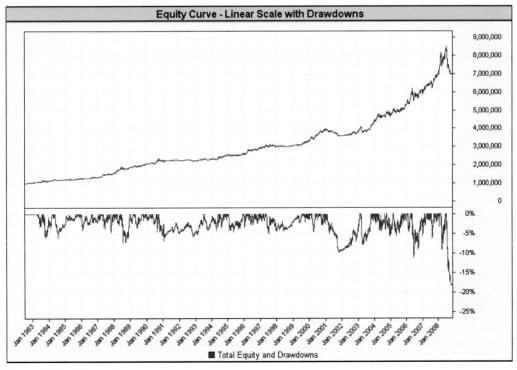

Source: Trading Blox LLC

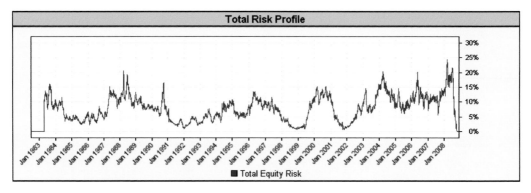

Source: Trading Blox LLC

Points to note

Unexciting

The severity of the recent collapse in commodity prices can be seen in the drawdown chart above – we are in the middle of the maximum drawdown. While long only investment in un-geared commodities is unexciting, commodities can add an important diversification benefit to a combined portfolio which includes stocks and many commodities are now available in convenient exchange traded form.

Preference for futures

Despite the convenience of ETCs, I would prefer to gain commodity exposure through the more liquid and diversified futures markets. The leverage offered by the futures markets offers far greater flexibility in terms of money management and of course the leverage offers the possibility of dialling up returns, should you wish to.

Convenience

Nonetheless, providing the liquidity is there and the spreads are reasonably tight, ETCs should offer the investor a way to diversify their portfolio without having to engage in the complications of the futures markets.

Trading short

Don't

As far as my tests show, as a long-term trend follower, the answer is, probably, "don't" – at least not with ETFs or ETCs. Using futures may be a different matter.

Why not?

This is not the place to enter a detailed argument as to why this might be the case but in terms of equities, the long-term bias is up and long-term trend profits are captured, in general, by long, smooth upwards movement rather than the often very rapid and difficult to capture down moves. Perhaps an additional disadvantage of shorting ETCs is that the collateral return gives an upwards bias to the investment that a position in the futures market would not. In the futures market, you are trading on price alone and benefiting separately from interest on your capital not needed for margin; with an ETC, the interest element is added daily to price.

Short ETCs

There are of course "short" ETFs and ETCs on offer, but for the long-term trend follower I really rather doubt that these are worth the extra risk, expense or effort. Certainly to borrow stock to short (even if it were available) would seem inadvisable.

Shorting equities

Bollinger Band Breakout Test 8 below applies the system to taking short trades only on Portfolio 1. No dividends accrue to stock sold short and to emphasise the profitability (or otherwise) of the actual trading, you will note that I have assumed no interest accruing on cash balances and no TER charged.

Bollinger Band breakout test 8: short trades only, portfolio I, equities

End balance	CAGR %	RAR %	Std dev	Annual Sharpe	Max total equity DD	Longest drawdown	Trades	RSquared
777,599	-0.87	-2.33	7.18	-0.34	54.2	316	555	79

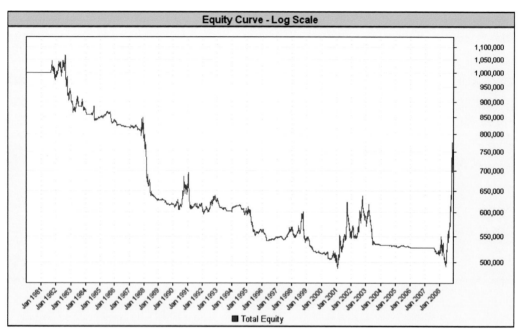

Source: Trading Blox LLC

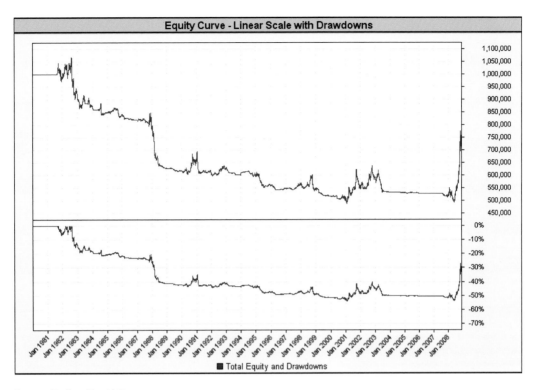

Source: Trading Blox LLC

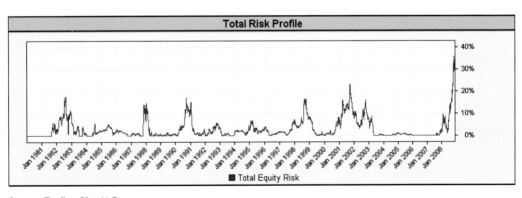

Source: Trading Blox LLC

Assumptions

Parameter	Value
Starting capital	USD1m
Start date	1st January 1980
End date	20th November 2008
Base currency	US dollars
Risk free rate	3%
Interest	None on un-invested balances
Costs & interest	No stock borrowing costs, no interest on short sales proceeds
Dividends	Price only indices used for equities, dividends are not accrued on short positions
Re-balancing	Quarterly
Margin	Any arising eliminated by sale of stock
Re-balance threshold	5%
Buffer	3%
Slippage	10%
Commission	Charged at 0.3% of the dollar value of the transaction
Annual fees	None charged

Points to note

Dismal

There is little point in commenting in detail on this dismal test. Note the profitability during the 2007 to (so far) 2008 bear market. It is doubtful that the system will be able to hold onto its gains and probable that the downturn in the equity curve will resume as stock markets recover.

Trading long and short

Combining short trades with long trades might be expected to add diversification: shorts might be expected to boost profits during market downturns. I can only report that in extensive testing using this system, no such benefits accrued: the system loses money on shorting stock and adding short trades to long trades merely detracted from the profitability of the latter.

Shorting commodities

Set out below are the test results for taking short only positions on the ETC proxies in Portfolio 2.

Bollinger Band breakout test 9: short trades only, commodities

End balance	CAGR %	RAR %	Std dev	Annual Sharpe	Max total equity DD	Longest drawdown	Trades	RSquared
1,093,288	0.34	-0.32	3.83	-0.45	20.9	184	801	25.37

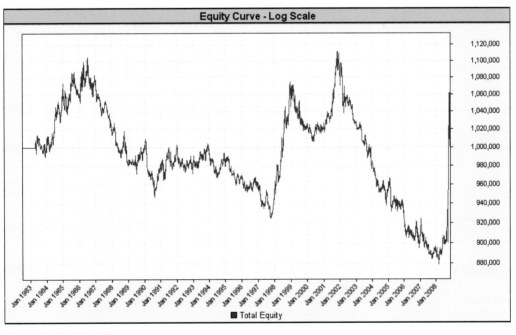

Source: Trading Blox LLC

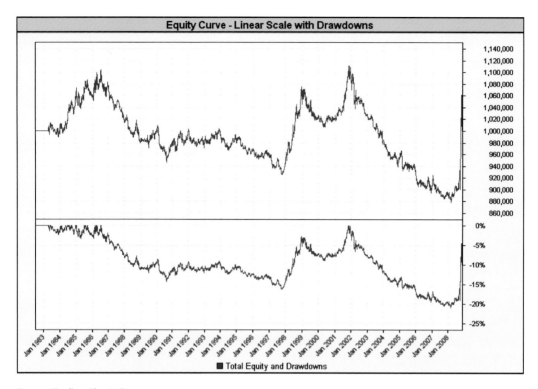

Source: Trading Blox LLC

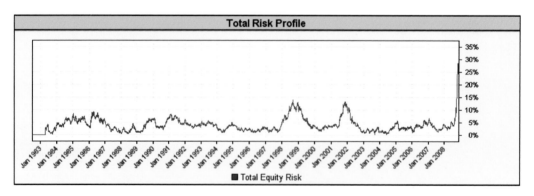

Source: Trading Blox LLC

Assumptions

Parameter	Value
Starting capital	USD1m
Start date	1st January 1980
End date	20th November 2008
Base currency	US dollars
Risk free rate	3%
Interest	None on un-invested balances
Costs & interest	No stock borrowing costs, no interest on short sales proceeds
Yield	Commodity indices include roll yield and collateral yield
Re-balancing	Quarterly
Margin	Any arising eliminated by sale of stock
Re-balance threshold	5%
Buffer	3%
Slippage	10%
Commission	Charged at 0.3% of the dollar value of the transaction
Annual fees	None charged

Points to note

Lacklustre

Again, there is little to comment on in this lacklustre test other than to note that shorting the commodities in Portfolio 1 has made a small profit for the period. It is clearly less disastrous to short commodities on a trend following basis than to short equities.

Trading long and short

It is sometimes the case that trading a marginally or only just profitable but uncorrelated system can actually add profit or reduce volatility. Given the particular portfolios I have used for the purposes of this chapter and the assumptions I have made, I can find no such benefit in adding short trades either of commodities or of equities or of the two in combination: shorting added considerable risk and provided scant or no benefit. Nor does a stepped parameter test, using different length moving averages and different band widths, show much benefit to be gained from using different parameters for short trades.

Bear market profitability

It is true that to have traded short in recent months would have been highly profitable but such periods are very much the exception rather than the rule.

Summary

- **Simple, robust and effective.** The Bollinger Band Breakout System has few rules, is simple to operate and is shown to be profitable over many different parameters and time periods.

- **Compares favourably to buy-and-hold.** The system has been shown to achieve superior risk adjusted performance to that of the buy-and-hold benchmark over a number of different portfolios.

- **Diversification adds benefits.** Adding bills and commodities may reduce absolute performance but can make for increased risk-adjusted performance and a smoother equity curve with shallower drawdowns.

- **Trading short adds little.** It is difficult to make much money trading short using a long-term trend following system, either on a standalone basis or in conjunction with long trades.

Increasing the Returns on the Bollinger Band Breakout System

The aims of this chapter are–

- **Increased returns.** To explore whether the returns on the Bollinger Band System can be enhanced.
- **Leverage.** To suggest that the use of leverage is not necessary in achieving higher returns.
- **Money management.** To look at using money management to increase returns.

Leverage

There are an increasing number of ETFs providing geared exposure to both the equity and commodity markets. Geared equity exposure however is mostly limited to the major markets. If your aim is wide global exposure then you are unlikely to find geared products for all the markets you wish to cover.

I am not sure how sensible or reasonable it is to borrow on margin to buy stocks for long-term investment. I would very much prefer not to. Many commentators and analysts give figures which assume leverage to produce exciting returns, but immodest gearing has become a dirty word after the disastrous events of the past few years. It is a double edged sword as many have discovered.

The leverage provided by the futures markets, if used in moderation, can do wonders for your performance without leading to jaw dropping drawdowns. To have to borrow money at a hefty spread over LIBOR to speculate on stocks is a very different matter.

The object of this chapter (and indeed that on the Momentum system to follow) is to suggest that leverage may not be necessary to ratchet up returns. There are other ways.

Regrettably, boosting the return of a system often involves increasing volatility and risk; higher rewards are usually accompanied in the financial world by increased perils. But for the investor who can stand the increased stress, the rewards are there.

Use of money management to increase returns

Concentration of account equity

The tests in this chapter will show that it is possible to increase the returns of this system by concentrating the available money in the account into stocks for which the system is showing a buy signal, rather than using the less concentrated money management method of dividing total account equity over the total universe of stocks in the potential portfolio.

System parameters

In the last chapter, you will recall the screen for the Bollinger Band Breakout system and the parameters "AlgorithMM" (set to "Trading Instruments") and "Minimum MMSignals" (set to "1"). My coding defines "Trading Instruments" as the number of instruments in the portfolio which are primed and trading on any given date.

Looking at Portfolio 1 in Appendix 1 you will see that the instrument for which I have the most data is the S&P 500, starting on 4th January 1980. The 200-day smoothed moving average for the S&P 500 is primed by 16th October 1980 and on that date, the number of "Trading Instruments" equals one. On that day, the S&P was trading above the Bollinger Band (the entry threshold) and a position was taken. Since on that date there was only one "Trading Instrument" and "Minimum MM Signals" was set to "1", the system invested the whole account balance in the S&P 500.

In the table below, you will see set out in the column headed "Trading Instruments", the dates when new instruments became available to trade – where there was sufficient trading data to prime the moving average. Using the money management algorithm "Trading Instruments", the portion of the total account equity devoted to any single trade is diluted as new instruments come on stream. The algorithm "Trading Instruments" divides the total account equity by the number of instruments which are primed on any given day.

Signals

In the Bollinger Band Breakout System, I coded an additional money management algorithm which I called "Signals". The column headed "Signals" in the table represents the number of instruments in Portfolio 1 trading on the given day above the entry threshold – above the upper Bollinger Band. This number will obviously always be less than or equal to "Trading Instruments" on that day.

	Signals	Trading Instruments
16/10/1980	1	1
23/10/1980	2	2
23/10/1981	1	3
03/07/1982	0	5
19/10/1982	2	6
28/10/1982	3	7
29/10/1982	3	8
13/10/1983	8	9
25/02/1984	9	10
21/05/1985	7	11
06/06/1986	10	12
24/07/1987	12	13
21/10/1987	8	14
18/10/1988	10	15
11/02/1989	14	16
13/06/1989	15	17
19/12/1989	15	18
03/01/1991	2	19
04/10/1991	11	20
22/10/1992	6	21
12/11/1993	19	22
30/09/1994	14	23
17/09/1997	20	24
06/08/1998	15	25
25/11/1999	21	26

Switching money management algorithm

By switching "AlgorithMM" to "Signals", the money management algorithm divides up total equity by the (most often smaller) number of "Signals" instead of the total number of "Trading Instruments", subject to the minimum defined by "Minimum MM Signals".

Thus this algorithm concentrates the portfolio by dividing up the total available equity into the number of stock trading on any given day above the entry threshold. This can make for better (or rather greater) returns than the more diluted algorithm "Trading Instruments".

Minimum MM signals

Setting "Minimum MM Signals" to "1" does not mean that the whole account is invested in one stock on every occasion. Looking at the table above, you will see that on most dates listed, there was more than just one "Signal" and on dates where there is more than one signal, the account equity will be invested equally in each signal. Equally, if "Minimum MM Signals" is set to 10, by way of example, this is a minimum only, and on 25th November 1999, as you can see from the above table, there were 21 instruments trading above the entry threshold: therefore the account would be spread over 21 investments.

Testing signals

The object of the test below is to see whether using the money management algorithm "Signals" produces an increased return when compared with the identical test run in the last chapter using the more diluted money management algorithm "Trading Instruments".

Bollinger Band breakout test 10: setting AlgorimMM to "signals" and minimum MM signals to "1"

End balance	CAGR%	RAR%	Std dev	Annual Sharpe	Max total equity DD	Longest drawdown	RSquared
159,709,979	19.18	20.51	15.89	0.71	37.4	37.8	95.49

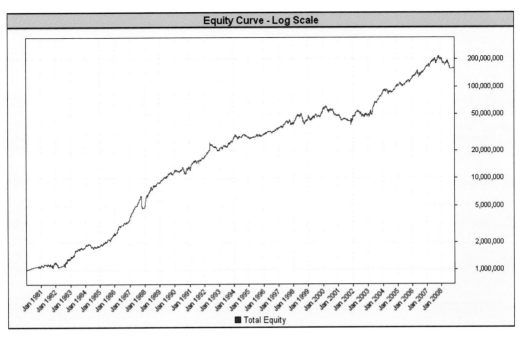

Source: Trading Blox LLC

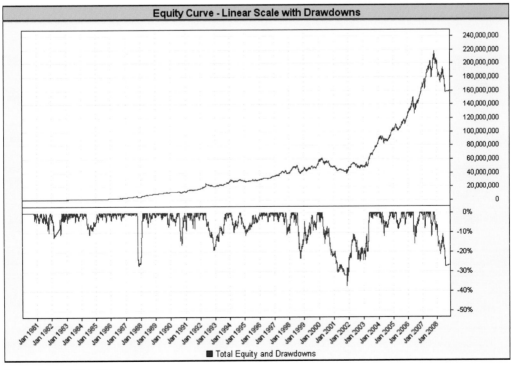

Source: Trading Blox LLC

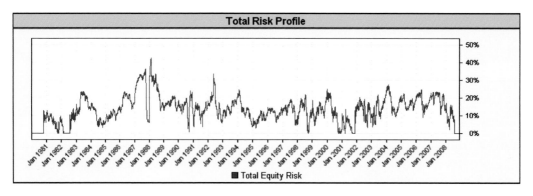

Source: Trading Blox LLC

Assumptions

Parameter	Value
Portfolio used	Portfolio 1 – Equities
Trades taken	Long only
Moving average	200 days
Entry threshold	1 std dev
Starting capital	USD1m
Start date	1st January 1980
End date	20th November 2008
MM algorithm	With signal
Minimum MM signals	1
Re-balance threshold	5%
Re-balance frequency	Quarterly
Eliminate margin	True. Any margin arising eliminated by sale of stock
Leverage	None
Buffer	3%
Base currency	US dollars
Risk free rate	3%
Annual fees	1.5% deducted
Interest	At the rate of three-month US Government T-Bills accrues on any un-invested balances
Dividends	Price only indices used but cash dividends are collected and re-invested quarterly
Slippage	10%
Commission	Charged at 0.3% of the dollar value of the transaction

Comparison table

For ease of comparison, I set out a table of relevant figures below:

	BBBO System "Trading Instruments"	BBBO System "Signals"	Buy and Hold
CAGR	14.12%	19.18%	12.7%
Risk adjusted CAGR	14.12%	12.84%	7.99%
RAR	13.99%	20.51%	15.86%
Risk adjusted RAR	13.99%	13.73%	9.98%
Max total equity drawdown	24%	37.4%	58.9%
Average max drawdown	16.68%	26.84%	38.4%
Longest drawdown	44.2 months	37.8 months	45.9 months
Average max drawdown length	22.17 months	19.80 months	38.54 months
Standard deviation	10.64	15.89	16.91
Winning months	252 (72.6%)	246 (70.89%)	226 (65%)
Losing months	95 (27.4%)	101 (29.1%)	121 (35%)

Points to note

CAGR/RAR

As can be seen, this more concentrated money management algorithm ("Signals") has greatly increased the level of absolute return over that obtained with the same system but using the less concentrated algorithm ("Trading Instruments").

Risk adjusted return

In terms of risk adjusted CAGR, the use of the algorithm "Signals" (at least in this test) produces an inferior return to the algorithm "Trading Instruments". The object however was to increase return without using leverage and to that extent, the experiment can be said to have succeeded. Note that risk adjusted RAR for each algorithm is similar.

Drawdown

As can be seen from the table above higher returns have come with a proportionately much greater increase in drawdowns. If a higher return is what you seek, then a higher drawdown is the price you are going to have to accept.

Standard deviation

Again, as can be expected, the volatility is considerably higher as a result of concentrating your firepower. Higher returns have come at higher risk.

Comparison to buy and hold

Even so, as can be seen from the table above, the BBBO System using the "Signals" algorithm compares very favourably to the buy-and-hold Benchmark. Considerably higher returns are achieved for less risk and lower drawdowns.

Stepping portfolio concentration over different time periods

Problem

Most people would be unhappy with too narrow a concentration of funds. It should also be noted that using the "Signals" money management algorithm is unlikely to outperform during every time period. It is useful therefore to run stepped parameter tests varying both the portfolio concentration and the time period.

Testing varied parameter settings

I set out below the results of stepped parameter tests (for three successive periods) using precisely the same assumptions as Bollinger Band Breakout Test 10 above, with the exception of start and end dates, and "Minimum MM Signals", which I have stepped from 1 to 15 by increments of 2.

Bollinger Band breakout test 11: stepping portfolio concentration

1st January 1980 to 29th December 1989

Min MM signals	Ending balance	CAGR (%)	MAR	Annual Sharpe	Equity DD	Longest DD	StdDev
1	11,942,112	28.15%	1.04	1.02	27.10%	12	15.6
3	11,247,084	27.38%	1.01	1.2	27.10%	12	14.0
5	10,107,605	26.03%	0.96	1.47	27.10%	12	13.2
7	9,409,800	25.13%	0.93	1.59	27.10%	13	12.9
9	8,531,084	23.91%	0.88	1.62	27.10%	15	12.4
11	7,486,303	22.30%	0.84	1.71	26.40%	16	11.6
13	6,478,309	20.54%	0.85	1.84	24.10%	16	10.4
15	5,802,914	19.22%	0.92	1.95	20.80%	15	9.2

29th December 1989 to 27th December 1999

Min MM signals	Ending balance	CAGR (%)	MAR	Annual Sharpe	Equity DD	Longest DD	StdDev
1	4,622,469	16.54%	0.72	1.15	22.90%	16	15.1
3	3,999,941	14.87%	0.64	0.97	23.10%	16	14.5
5	3,793,634	14.26%	0.65	0.93	22.00%	17	14.4
7	3,711,358	14.01%	0.65	0.92	21.60%	17	14.3
9	3,628,103	13.75%	0.65	0.89	21.30%	17	14.1
11	3,516,058	13.40%	0.63	0.9	21.40%	17	13.7
13	3,403,631	13.03%	0.6	0.9	21.70%	17	13.1
15	3,324,382	12.76%	0.6	0.9	21.40%	17	12.6

27th December 1999 to 20th November 2008

Min MM signals	Ending balance	CAGR (%)	MAR	Annual Sharpe	Equity DD	Longest DD	StdDev
1	2,649,251	11.55%	0.31	0.32	36.70%	38	15.7
3	2,424,991	10.44%	0.32	0.3	32.50%	41	14.3
5	2,235,631	9.44%	0.29	0.28	32.20%	43	13.2
7	2,222,275	9.37%	0.32	0.3	28.90%	44	12.5
9	2,225,530	9.39%	0.35	0.32	26.60%	44	11.9
11	2,250,828	9.53%	0.38	0.34	25.00%	44	11.6
13	2,271,178	9.64%	0.4	0.35	23.80%	44	11.4
15	2,301,717	9.80%	0.43	0.37	23.00%	44	11.1

Comparison to "trading instruments" algorithm

To save having to look back to Bollinger Band Breakout Test 5 in the previous chapter, here are the results again for the BBBO System using exactly the same parameters except for the money management algorithm which was as follows: "AlgorithMM" (set to "Trading Instruments") and "Minimum MMSignals" (set to "1").

Ending balance	CAGR (%)	Annual Sharpe	Max equity DD	Longest DD	StdDev
1st January 1980 to 29th December 1989					
6,497,608	20.58	1.41	24	16	11.7
29th December 1989 to 27th December 1999					
2,933,916	11.36	0.96	13.6	23	10.01
27th December 1999 to 20th November 2008					
2,326,900	9.93	0.47	16.9	44	9.47

Points to note

More gain

Investing the whole account in those funds which are trading above the entry threshold at any given time, can considerably increase the return, at least in absolute terms.

More pain

Increased drawdown and volatility are the price to be paid for the higher return.

More volatility

A more concentrated money management approach tends to soar higher and dip lower. It generally has more exposure to the market.

Summary

- **Return**. The absolute return of the Bollinger Band Breakout System can be increased without the use of leverage by concentrating the whole of account equity in stocks for which "Buy" signals are indicated.

- **Downside**. Volatility and drawdown are increased to a proportionately greater extent than return.

- **Benchmark comparison**. An investor may nonetheless be able to achieve significantly higher returns than those available from the buy-and-hold benchmark, both on an absolute and risk adjusted basis.

A Momentum System

The aims of this chapter are–

- **Description of system**. To describe in detail another long-term trading system.

- **Increased returns**. To explore the possibility of achieving higher returns than those of the enhanced Bollinger Band Breakout System, again without the use of leverage.

- **Equal treatment of equities and commodities**. To explore the benefits of giving equal weight to a mixed portfolio of equities and commodities.

- **Trading short**. To ascertain whether this system can reap any benefit from short trading.

Description of the system

General

This system ranks funds in a universe of potential investments on an end of month basis by performance. The best performers are those which have recorded the greatest rise as at the relevant month end for the period being measured. The worst performers are those which have recorded the greatest decline. The portfolio is then adjusted at the open at the beginning of the immediately following month based on these performance rankings. You must choose a portfolio concentration level: how many stocks or funds do you wish to hold in your portfolio at any one time? Let us call this number X.

Rules for long trades

- **Entry**. Subject to the Filter (see below), at the beginning of each month buy at the open the top X performing funds (or rather any of the top X performing funds that you do not already hold).

- **Exit**. At the beginning of each month sell at the open any funds you hold which no longer rank amongst the top X performing funds.

Rules for short trades

- **Entry**. Subject to the Filter (see below), at the beginning of each month sell short at the open the worst X performing funds (or any of the worst X performing funds that you have not already sold short).

- **Exit**. At the beginning of each month buy back at the open any funds you hold which no longer rank in the worst X performing funds.

Money management

The money management algorithm invests total account value, divided by X, in each *new* position. When trading both long and short, the account equity will be divided by X (long stocks) + X (short stocks).

Parameters

It is helpful to look at a screenshot for this system:

Global Parameters	Momentum	

Portfolio Manager ▲

○ Futures		
● Stocks	Dividend Stocks ▼	
○ Forex		
Trade Direction	Trade Long ▼	
Lookback 1	Step ☐	260
Lookback 2	Step ☐	130
Lookback 3	Step ☐	60
Lookback 4	Step ☐	20
Choose Momentum Calculation	All ▼	
Filter Type	MA Crossover ▼	
Long Term Filter	Step ☐	200
Short Term Filter	Step ☐	50

Entries and Exits ▲

Rebalance Threshold	Step ☐	5%
Rebalance Frequency	None ▼	
Eliminate Margin	True ▼	
MM Equity	Trading Equity ▼	
Percentage Commission	Step ☐	0.3%
Leverage	Step ☐	1
Debug	None ▼	
Debug Start Date		20080101
Debug End Date		20081120
Max Long Instruments	Step ☐	10
Max Short Instruments	Step ☐	1
Buffer	Step ☐	3%

Risk Manager ▼

Auxiliary ▲

Monthly Incentive (%)	Step ☐	0%
Net Assets (%)	Step ☐	1.5%
Charge Fees	True ▼	

Source: Trading Blox LLC

Below are some notes on the parameters shown in the screenshot.

Lookback

Lookback 1, 2, 3 and 4 are expressed in days and used in the performance calculation for each instrument at each month end. The first performance measurement (based on the above parameter settings) will take the current closing price of the relevant instrument and divide it by the close as at the beginning of the 260-day "lookback" period. Three further performance calculations are made, using the periods specified in the other "lookback" parameter settings. Thus instrument performance is calculated over, roughly, 12, 6, 3 and 1-month periods.

Choose momentum calculation

The parameter "Choose Momentum Calculation" is set to "All". On this setting, the four performance calculations for each stock described in "lookback" above are added together and divided by four to give an average performance measurement. The stocks are then ranked on this average, to arrive at the top or bottom X performing instruments at the end of each month. Other settings for this parameter allow testing for a single lookback period or any combination but I have generally found "All" the most satisfactory for my purposes and shall concentrate on that setting for this chapter.

Filter

The system can be run with or without a filter. If no filter is used, the account is fully invested at all times in the top/bottom X stocks. If the filter is used, then there will be periods where less than X positions are held and the balance is held in short-term bills or cash. In stark contrast to the position of a buy and hold investment, the filter gives an escape route into the safety of cash in times of trouble.

Filter type

The "Filter Type" which I concentrate on in this chapter is a Dual Moving Average Crossover. The long-term moving average is a simple moving average of the closing price of the instrument over the period of days chosen in "Long Term Filter". The short-term moving average is calculated using the number of days chosen in "Short Term Filter".

No new long position is taken in respect of any given instrument unless:

1. the most recent closing price of that instrument is above the most recent short moving average calculation; and

2. the short moving average is above the long moving average.

If an existing position is ranked in the top X but fails the filter test, that stock will nonetheless be sold. The reverse logic applies to short positions.

Max long instruments, max short instruments

This is where to set the value of X. "Max Long Instruments" set to 10 means that the system will invest (filter permitting) in the top ten ranked instruments. "Max Short Instruments" set to 1 would cause investment in the single worst performer in the portfolio. Where both long and short positions are taken, the money management algorithm adds both Max Long Instruments and Short Instruments together (to make 11 in this example) and 1/11th of the account value will be invested in a new position.

MM equity

Tests in this chapter leave "MM Equity" set on "Trading Equity" (the entire account value).

Re-balance frequency

Unless you choose the option to re-balance on a monthly basis, you will have unequal holdings in some of your X stocks. The money management algorithm only operates for new positions. No re-balancing is used for the tests in this chapter. Re-balancing did not prove particularly valuable in a system which turns over its investments on a fairly frequent basis – so "Re-balance Frequency" is left on the setting "None".

Eliminate margin

The frequent turnover of stocks with this system prevents much of a build up of margin. There is normally enough free cash in the account to take on new positions as old positions are sold. Nevertheless, "Eliminate Margin" was set to "True" for the tests in this chapter and on the odd occasion when margin arises, stock is sold down proportionately.

Buffer

A "Buffer" of 3% is deducted from the amount which would otherwise be invested in a new position – this helps to ensure that no margin is incurred and that cash is left in the account to pay expenses.

Debug

Ignore this. These provisions are simply used to help sort out problems when designing or altering the system.

Charge Fees

I have again provided in the tests in this chapter for annual fees of 1.5% of the total value of the account to be charged by way of estimation of the total expense ratio and tracking error which might be expected over a broad range of index tracking ETFs.

Test start and end dates

There is little point testing this system on Portfolio 1 on a standalone basis with a start date prior to 1st January 1991. It is not until this date that there is a sensible number of equity indices with sufficient data to prime a 200-day moving average (18). To test prior to that date would make little sense, since the object of the system is to choose the best performers out of a number of different indices. By 1st January 1991, Portfolio 2 provides 26 commodities with sufficient data to prime a 200-day moving average and so that is also a reasonable date to commence a test for commodities.

Code available for download

I have posted this system (coded for Trading Blox) under the heading "Blox Market Place" on the Trading Blox Forum. Users of Trading Blox can download the system for free for as long as the proprietor of Trading Blox keeps the website and my post in existence.

Testing the equities portfolio

Set out below are the test results for the Momentum system on a long only test of Portfolio 1, the equities portfolio.

Momentum test 1: 1st January 1991 to 20th November 2008, portfolio 1, equities, long only

End balance	CAGR %	RAR %	Std dev	Annual Sharpe	Max total equity DD	Longest drawdown (months)	Trades	RSquared
8,732,962	12.86	12.17	12.37	0.64	18.2	42.8	463	93.44

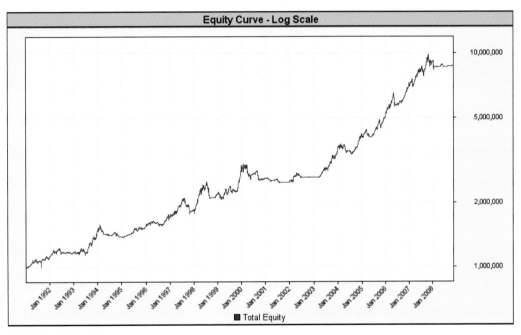

Source: Trading Blox LLC

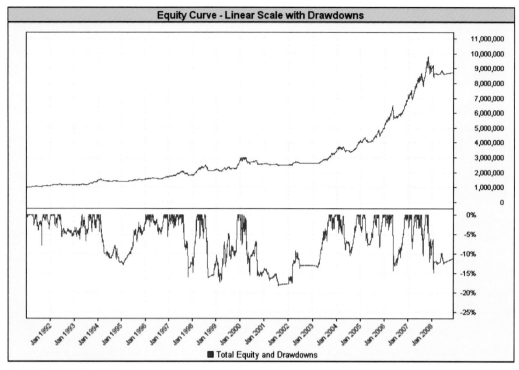

Source: Trading Blox LLC

Assumptions

Parameter	Value
Starting capital	USD1m
Start date	1st January 1991
End date	20th November 2008
Momentum calculation	All
Max long instruments	10
Re-balance threshold	5%
Re-balance frequency	None
Eliminate margin	True. Any margin arising eliminated by sale of stock
Leverage	None
Buffer	3%
Base currency	US dollars
Risk free rate	3%
Annual fees	1.5% deducted
Interest	At the rate of three-month US Government T-Bills accrues on any un-invested balances
Dividends	Price only indices used but cash dividends are collected and re-invested quarterly
Slippage	10%
Commission	0.3% of the dollar value of the transaction

Comparison table

For comparison, I set out a table of relevant figures below. The BBBO System was run using the money management algorithm "Signals" with "Minimum MM Signals" set to 15.

	Bollinger Band Breakout	Buy and Hold	Momentum
CAGR	12.20%	8.82%	12.86%
Risk adjusted CAGR	12.20%	6.24%	12.75%
RAR	11.16%	11.5%	12.17%
Risk adjusted RAR	11.16%	8.14%	12.06%
Max total equity drawdown	23.30%	58.9%	18.2%
Average max drawdown	18.60%	32.78%	16.14%
Longest drawdown	44.2 months	45.9 months	42.8
Average max drawdown length	20.94 months	18.07 months	21.13
Standard deviation	12.26	17.33	12.37
Winning months	142 (66%)	135 (62.8%)	145 (67.4%)
Losing months	73 (34%)	37.2 (37.2%)	70 (32.6%)
Winning trades	863 (71.8%)	714 (75.7%)	283 (61.6%)
Losing trades	329 (28.2%)	229 (24.3%)	180 (38.9%)

Points to note

CAGR

The Momentum System records a useful pick up in absolute return over the enhanced BBBO System and a considerably higher return than buy-and-hold. Buy-and-hold reached an equity peak of around $11m in October 2007 while the BBBO and Momentum systems each reached a high of just under $10m – as usual, buy-and-hold is seen rising higher and plunging far lower. This highlights the greater sensitivity of buy-and-hold to start and end dates. If an end date in October 2007 had been used, buy-and-hold would have had a significant lead in absolute return. In terms of risk adjusted return however, each system has a clear and very significant advantage over the buy-and-hold benchmark.

RAR

RAR is helpful in emphasising the performance of buy-and-hold in a manner less sensitive to start and end dates: in absolute terms its performance looks healthy. However, the Momentum System is the clear winner in this test.

Drawdown

As expected, the Momentum System suffers very much lower drawdowns than buy-and-hold. As with the BBBO System, the Momentum System has the enormous advantage of exiting the market during times of crisis. The psychological advantage of having strict criteria for staying away from the markets is enormous. So often the supposed buy-and-hold investor proves incapable of living through a bear market and sells when he can stand the pain no longer. This guarantees that his loss will be permanent.

Trades

The Momentum System records only 463 trades as opposed to 1,192 for the BBBO System. The latter system, using the "With Signals" algorithm, requires frequent sales of stock to eliminate margin as new trades are taken. Fewer trades mean less effort and less chance of un-forecast slippage and other frictional costs.

Advantage over buy and hold

The relative merits of the BBBO and the Momentum systems are subject to variations depending on the parameters used, portfolios and time frames. It is far more important to focus on the great superiority of each system over buy-and-hold. The huge drawdowns and greatly increased volatility of buy-and-hold make either of the two mechanical systems look extremely attractive by comparison.

Testing the commodities portfolio

The following back-test shows the performance of the Momentum System, long only trades, on Portfolio 2, Commodities.

Momentum test 2: 1st January 1991 to 20th November 2008, portfolio 2, long only

End balance	CAGR %	RAR %	Std dev	Annual Sharpe	Max total equity DD	Longest drawdown	Trades	RSquared
7,750,389	12.11	11.57	13.78	0.64	22	32.2	511	91.91

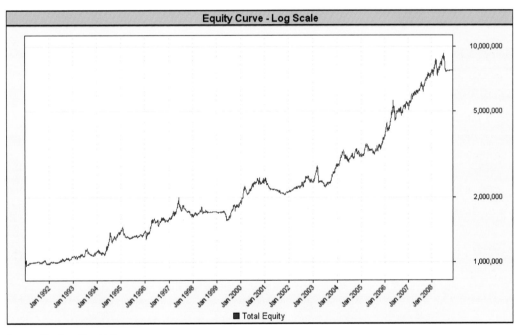

Source: Trading Blox LLC

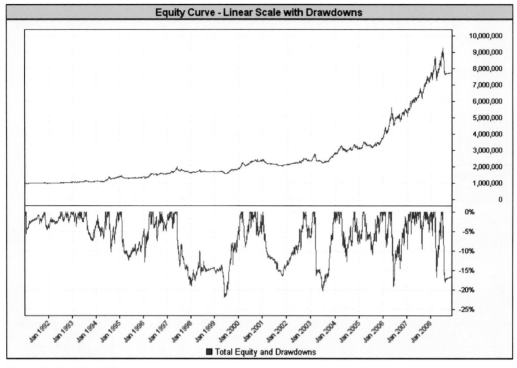

Source: Trading Blox LLC

Assumptions

Parameter	Value
Starting capital	USD1m
Start date	1st January 1991
End date	20th November 2008
Momentum calculation	All
Max long instruments	10
Re-balance threshold	5%
Re-balance frequency	None
Eliminate margin	True. Any margin arising eliminated by sale of stock
Leverage	None
Buffer	3%
Base currency	US dollars
Risk free rate	3%
Annual fees	1.5% deducted
Interest	At the rate of three-month US Government T-Bills accrues on any un-invested balances
Dividends	Price only indices used but cash dividends are collected and re-invested quarterly
Slippage	10%
Commission	0.3% of the dollar value of the transaction

Comparison Table

For comparison, I set out a table of relevant figures below. The BBBO System was run using the money management algorithm "Signals" with "Minimum MM Signals" set to 15.

	Bollinger Band Breakout	Buy and Hold	Momentum
CAGR	8.24%	3.97%	12.11%
Risk adjusted CAGR	8.24%	3.87%	9.45%
RAR	8.94%	6.19%	11.57%
Risk adjusted RAR	8.94%	6.03%	9.03%
Max total equity drawdown	25.2%	43.5%	22%
Average max drawdown	17.09%	22.25%	19.25%
Longest drawdown	29.7 months	36 months	32.2 months
Average max drawdown length	15.15 months	16.12 months	21.13 months
Standard deviation	10.76	11.05	13.78
Winning months	132 (61.4%)	130 (60.5%)	137 (63.7%)
Losing months	83 (38.6%)	85 (39.5%)	78 (36.3%)
Winning trades	867 (62%)	932 (79.2%)	247 (48.3%)
Losing trades	532 (38%)	245 (20.8%)	264 (51.7%)

Points to note

CAGR

Concentration on outperformers has enabled the Momentum System to outperform both buy-and-hold and the BBBO System in both absolute and risk adjusted terms. The Momentum System has achieved a greater return than the enhanced BBBO System without the use of leverage.

RAR

Of particular interest is the much lower RAR for the buy-and-hold approach. On this portfolio of commodities, buy-and-hold fails to approach the equity highs reached by the two mechanical systems: $3.5m as opposed to $5.5m for the BBBO System and over $9m for the Momentum System.

Portfolio concentration

In markets where there is no upwards bias, it pays high dividends to concentrate in the best performing markets while ignoring the rest. The enhanced BBBO System will often be invested in more than the "Minimum MM Signals" of 15 commodities, since there are 27 commodities in the portfolio. In sharp contrast, the Momentum System concentrates each month on the ten best performing commodities in the portfolio.

Drawdown

As usual, the maximum loss in peak to valley account value is greatly reduced by the use of a system.

Testing bills, equities and commodities

In Test 3 below, we look at would happen if the system trades Portfolio 1 (equities – with an allocation of 60%), Portfolio 2 (commodities – with an allocation of 20%), leaving an allocation to short-term bills of 20%.

Even though the Momentum System as tested here uses no re-balancing, the frequent turnover in the portfolio at each month end ensures that the 60/20/20 split is loosely maintained.

Momentum test 3: 1st January 1991 to 20th November 2008, equities/commodities/bills, long only

End balance	CAGR %	RAR %	Std dev	Annual Sharpe	Max total equity DD	Longest drawdown (months)	Trades	RSquared
6,255,882	10.78	10.18	8.69	0.75	11.8	40.7	961	94.26

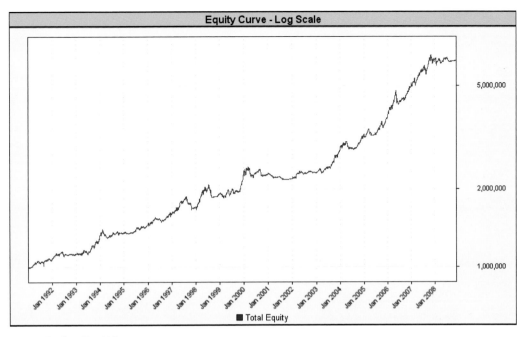

Source: Trading Blox LLC

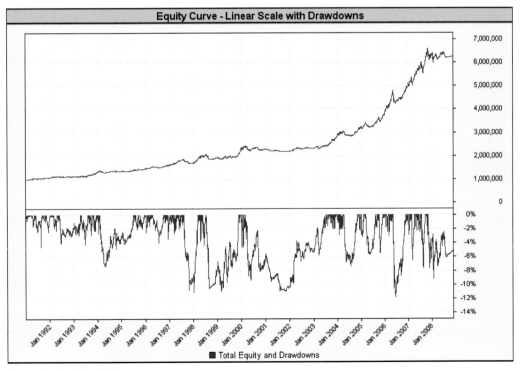

Source: Trading Blox LLC

Assumptions

Parameter	Value
Starting capital	USD1m
Start date	1st January 1991
End date	20th November 2008
Momentum calculation	All
Max long instruments	10
Re-balance threshold	5%
Re-balance frequency	None
Eliminate margin	True. Any margin arising eliminated by sale of stock
Leverage	None
Buffer	3%
Base currency	US dollars
Risk free rate	3%
Annual fees	1.5% deducted
Interest	At the rate of three-month US Government T-Bills accrues on any un-invested balances
Dividends	Price only indices used but cash dividends are collected and re-invested quarterly
Slippage	10%
Commission	0.3% of the dollar value of the transaction

Comparison table

For comparison, I set out a table of relevant figures below. The BBBO System was run using the money management algorithm "Signals" with "Minimum MM Signals" set to 15.

	Bollinger Band Breakout	Buy and Hold	Momentum
CAGR	9.67%	6.92%	10.78%
Risk adjusted CAGR	9.67%	4.99%	10.11%
RAR	9.14%	8.79%	10.18%
Risk adjusted RAR	9.14%	6.33%	9.55%
Max total equity drawdown	13.4%	43%	11.8%
Average max drawdown	11.76%	22.42%	10.84%
Longest drawdown	42.2 months	44.3 months	40.7 months
Average max drawdown length	19.06 moths	17.62 months	19.48 months
Standard deviation	8.15	11.31	8.69
Winning months	144 (67%)	141 (65.6%)	147 (68.4%)
Losing months	71 (33%)	74 (34.4%)	68 (31.6%)
Winning Trades	2377 (64.6%)	2689 (60.1%)	514 (53.5%)
Losing Trades	1305 (35.4%)	1784 (39.9%)	447 (46.5%)

Points to note

CAGR/RAR

Once again, the Momentum System comes in ahead on both in absolute and risk adjusted returns. While such figures are certainly not conclusive, it should certainly encourage the further investigation of such apparent superiority on other portfolios, parameters and time frames.

Drawdown

Each system greatly reduces the pain and anxiety of the very high loss in account equity suffered by followers of the buy-and-hold approach.

Treating equities and commodities equally

A new approach

So far in this book tests involving both equities and commodities have involved an asset allocation of 60% to equities, 20% to commodities and 20% to short-term bills. The approach in this section represents a radical departure in that Portfolio 3 combines both Portfolio 1 (equities) and Portfolio 2 (commodities) into one portfolio with no fixed allocation to short term bills. Equities and commodities are thus treated on an equal basis.

A significant advantage for the momentum system

For much of the period covered by the test set out below, the Momentum System has a choice of 26 equity indices and 27 commodities to invest in. Using Portfolio 3, the system takes the ten hottest markets each month, whether the Brazilian stock market, or gold or wheat. At times, all ten investments may be wholly in stocks, or commodities, or cash. At other times the system will be invested in a mixture.

By contrast

The buy-and-hold benchmark by contrast holds all components of the combined portfolio at all times (assuming sufficient data). Equally, the enhanced BBBO System can not "choose" what to invest in: it will merely divide its capital between such counters as are showing a "Buy" signal subject to a minimum divisor of 15.

Momentum test 4: 1st January 1991 to 20th November 2008, portfolio 3, long only

End balance	CAGR %	RAR %	Std dev	Annual Sharpe	Max total equity DD	Longest drawdown	Trades	RSquared
13,706,568	15.73	14.51	15.18	0.74	20.8	30.1	695	94.11

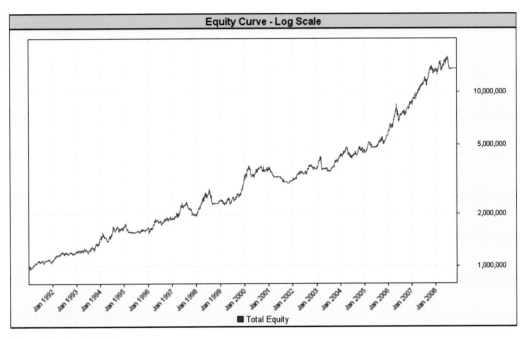

Source: Trading Blox LLC

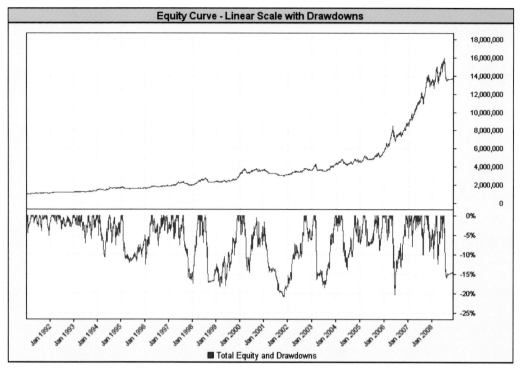

Source: Trading Blox LLC

Assumptions

Parameter	Value
Starting capital	USD1m
Start date	1st January 1991
End date	20th November 2008
Momentum calculation	All
Max long instruments	10
Re-balance threshold	5%
Re-balance frequency	None
Eliminate margin	True. Any margin arising eliminated by sale of stock
Leverage	None
Buffer	3%
Base currency	US dollars
Risk free rate	3%
Annual fees	1.5% deducted
Interest	At the rate of three-month US Government T-Bills accrues on any un-invested balances
Dividends	Price only indices used but cash dividends are collected and re-invested quarterly
Slippage	10%
Commission	0.3% of the dollar value of the transaction

Comparison table

For comparison, I set out a table of relevant figures below. The BBBO System was run using the money management algorithm "Signals" with "Minimum MM Signals" set to 15.

	Bollinger Band Breakout	Buy and Hold	Momentum
CAGR	10.48%	6.52%	15.73%
Risk adjusted CAGR	10.48%	6.08%	11.64%
RAR	10.28%	9.06%	14.51%
Risk adjusted RAR	10.28%	8.45%	10.74%
Max total equity drawdown	23.3%	48.1%	20.8%
Average max drawdown	18.6%	23.61%	19.10%
Longest drawdown	36.9 months	37.1 months	30.1 months
Average max drawdown length	16.36 months	16.83 months	15.61 months
Standard deviation	11.24	12.05	15.18
Winning months	140 (65.1%)	135 (62.8%)	133 (61.9%)
Losing months	75 (34.9%)	80 (37.2%)	82 (38.1%)
Winning trades	2801 (67.5%)	1634 (80.2%)	395 (56.8%)
Losing trades	1349 (32.5%)	403 (19.8%)	300 (43.2%)

Points to note

CAGR / RAR

The Momentum System comes into its own with this combined portfolio by concentrating on the ten hottest markets each month, whether equities or commodities. Adjusting the higher return of this system to the lower standard deviation of the enhanced BBBO System reduces its lead but returns have been substantially increased without the use of leverage.

Drawdown

Once again it can be seen that the use of a system greatly reduces drawdown.

Comparison between 60/20/20 Split and Portfolio 3 approach

	Momentum 60/20/20	Momentum Portfolio 3
CAGR	10.78%	15.73%
Risk adjusted CAGR	10.11%	9.00%
RAR	10.18%	14.51%
Risk adjusted RAR	9.55%	8.31%
Max total equity drawdown	11.8%	20.8%
Average max drawdown	10.84%	19.10%
Longest drawdown	40.7 months	30.1 months
Average max drawdown length	19.48 months	15.61 months
Standard deviation	8.69	15.18
Winning months	147 (68.4%)	133 (61.9%)
Losing months	68 (31.6%)	82 (38.1%)
Winning trades	514 (53.5%)	395 (56.8%)
Losing Trades	447 (46.5%)	300 (43.2%)

Comment

As can be seen from the table above, in many respects the logical investor should ignore the "equal treatment" approach tested in this section in favour of allocating the portfolio between equities, commodities and bills. In risk adjusted terms, the 60/20/20 approach is clearly superior and the drawdowns are far less severe. But if raw returns are required, the equal treatment approach gives the desired affect.

Stepped parameter tests

Parameters

You can of course choose to optimise any of the parameters of the system but, satisfied with the reasonable job done by the filter, I shall concentrate on showing the effect of varying "Max Long Instruments".

Time periods

The first test run set out below steps "Max Long Instruments" for the period 1st January 1991 to 11th November 2008.

The second test steps "Max Long Instruments" for successive five-year periods within the range 1st January 1984 to 20th November 2008. By 1st January 1984 there are 30 instruments with sufficient trading data in the combined Portfolio 3: not sufficient (and weighted towards commodities), but perhaps of interest nonetheless.

Momentum Test 5: 1st January 1991 to 20th November 2008, Portfolio 3, Stepping "Max Long Instruments", Long Only

Max long instruments	Ending balance	CAGR (%)	MAR	Annual Sharpe	Max total equity DD	Longest DD (mnth)	Trades	StdDev	Win duration	Loss duration
1	4,973,912	9.37%	0.13	0.18	73%	86	97	43	72	42
3	9,693,675	13.52%	0.28	0.37	49%	37	289	26	97	40
5	12,743,765	15.26%	0.43	0.56	36%	35	441	20	98	43
7	12,989,242	15.39%	0.57	0.62	27%	35	534	18	105	45
9	14,231,141	15.98%	0.72	0.73	22%	29	640	16	110	46
11	13,020,051	15.40%	0.75	0.72	21%	29	709	15	116	46
13	11,690,286	14.71%	0.73	0.8	20%	29	780	14	121	49
15	11,443,746	14.57%	0.76	0.85	19%	35	846	13	120	50
17	10,098,828	13.78%	0.76	0.79	18%	35	899	12	125	50
19	9,040,169	13.08%	0.78	0.77	17%	35	951	12	128	50
21	8,044,291	12.34%	0.77	0.75	16%	35	1015	11	132	50
23	7,377,460	11.80%	0.76	0.75	16%	35	1068	10	134	50
25	6,844,252	11.33%	0.76	0.74	15%	35	1109	10	138	50

Assumptions

Except where stated otherwise, the same as for Momentum Test 1.

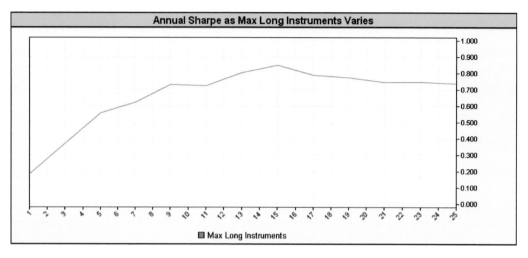

Source: Trading Blox LLC

Points to note

Optimal choice

Both the chart and table above suggest that in terms of this portfolio and timeframe, somewhere in the range of 10 to 15 Max Long Instruments looks a sensible choice; a reasonable trade off perhaps between risk and return. Return is highest within these parameters while maximum drawdown and standard deviation are within tolerable limits. When testing much larger portfolios I have found the most satisfactory number tends to stretch out towards 25.

Portfolio turnover

Trade duration is much shorter with this system when compared to the Bollinger Band Breakout. A good proportion of the portfolio turns over each month in search of the best performance, and profits are not allowed to "run" to the same extent. Win Duration to Loss Duration is around 4:1 on the Bollinger Band Tests; here the ratio is more like 2.4:1 at 15 "Max Long Instruments". Equally, there tend to be more losing trades with this system as non-performing trades are cut short.

Returns

As can be seen, without the use of any margin facility, the returns can be dialled up to increase return before over-concentration leads to diminishing performance.

Momentum test 6: 1st January 1984 to 20th November 2008 stepping both "Max Long Instruments" and "Start/End Dates", portfolio 3, long only

1st January 1984 to 30th December 1988

Max long instruments	Ending balance	CAGR (%)	MAR	Annual Sharpe	Max total equity DD	Longest DD (mnth)	Trades	StdDev	Win duration	Loss duration
5	3,890,696	31.22%	1.07	0.85	29%	15	124	26	97	44
10	3,376,016	27.55%	1.22	1.35	23%	11	189	18	115	45
15	2,754,362	22.46%	1.53	1.53	15%	8	209	13	132	50
20	2,577,814	20.85%	1.69	1.61	12%	8	213	11	145	51
25	2,314,863	18.28%	1.76	1.69	10%	6	223	9	147	51

30th December 1988 to 29th December 1993

Max long instruments	Ending balance	CAGR (%)	MAR	Annual Sharpe	Max total equity DD	Longest DD (mnth)	Trades	StdDev	Win duration	Loss duration
5	1,941,006	14.18%	0.75	0.88	19%	60	142	17	107	38
10	1,928,191	14.03%	1.15	1.03	12%	13	187	10	111	48
15	1,713,150	11.37%	1.31	0.89	9%	13	228	8	131	48
20	1,595,277	9.79%	1.51	0.82	7%	8	266	7	133	49
25	1,561,027	9.31%	1.8	0.79	5%	7	276	6	145	52

29th December 1993 to 28th December 1998

Max long instruments	Ending balance	CAGR (%)	MAR	Annual Sharpe	Max total equity DD	Longest DD (mnth)	Trades	StdDev	Win duration	Loss duration
5	1,745,996	11.79%	0.45	0.75	26%	60	137	17	78	42
10	1,630,308	10.27%	0.59	0.82	17%	15	210	12	108	44
15	1,621,670	10.15%	0.64	1.01	16%	11	263	10	113	47
20	1,559,035	9.29%	0.64	1.06	15%	11	289	9	130	48
25	1,454,891	7.79%	0.58	0.91	14%	8	320	7	148	48

28th December 1998 to 27th December 2003

Max long instruments	Ending balance	CAGR (%)	MAR	Annual Sharpe	Max total equity DD	Longest DD (mnth)	Trades	StdDev	Win duration	Loss duration
5	1,805,242	12.54%	0.34	0.33	37%	60	139	23	84	43
10	1,656,486	10.62%	0.52	0.45	20%	24	212	16	88	48
15	1,766,661	12.05%	0.71	0.59	17%	30	243	14	94	54
20	1,633,849	10.32%	0.77	0.56	14%	35	273	11	106	54
25	1,555,848	9.24%	0.8	0.54	12%	35	309	10	111	53

27th December 2003 to 20th November 2008

Max long instruments	Ending balance	CAGR (%)	MAR	Annual Sharpe	Max total equity DD	Longest DD (mnth)	Trades	StdDev	Win duration	Loss duration
5	2,432,498	19.82%	0.94	0.63	21%	60	152	23	99	47
10	3,145,566	26.25%	1.35	1	20%	7	245	17	111	50
15	2,992,482	24.97%	1.46	1.22	17%	8	283	15	128	54
20	2,537,566	20.85%	1.35	1.02	15%	8	314	14	125	52
25	2,319,535	18.66%	1.33	1	14%	8	334	13	137	52

Assumptions: except where stated otherwise, the same as for Momentum Test 1

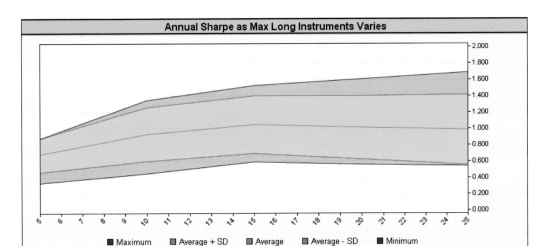

Source: Trading Blox LLC

Comment

Much the same conclusions can be drawn as for the previous test stepped parameter test. On this portfolio the system seems robust over a wide range of different parameters and different time periods.

Trading short

Profitable?

This chapter would not be complete without some comment on how well the system trades the short side.

The answer is, it doesn't, either alone or in combination with long trades. So far as concerns the portfolios I have tested, the parameters I have used and the assumptions I have made, taking short trades is a waste of time, effort and money. There are of course times when trading short brings profit, but in long-term trend following in general I am hard pushed to find much benefit in trading short, especially with equities.

Test results

I set out the test results using the same parameters using an expanded portfolio and taking short trades only. In terms of assumptions, I have assumed no dividends, no interest on unused balances and no annual management fees. I have also assumed no borrowing costs and no interest received on short sales.

Momentum test 7: stepping "max short instruments" and start/end dates, large portfolio, short only

1st January 1984 to 30th December 1988

Max short instruments	Ending balance	CAGR (%)	Mar	Max total DD	Longest DD (mnth)	Trades	StdDev	Win duration	Loss duration
5	828,973	-3.68%	-0.11	33%	42	121	9	55	19
15	867,460	-2.80%	-0.14	20%	46	262	5	53	23
25	910,158	-1.86%	-0.15	12%	53	326	4	46	20
35	940,175	-1.23%	-0.13	9%	46	346	3	44	20
45	953,854	-0.94%	-0.13	7%	46	354	2	43	20
55	962,184	-0.77%	-0.13	6%	46	354	2	43	20

30th December 1988 to 29th December 1993

Max short instruments	Ending balance	CAGR (%)	Mar	Max total DD	Longest DD (mnth)	Trades	StdDev	Win duration	Loss duration
5	892,827	-2.24%	-0.08	29%	60	155	13	63	27
15	956,568	-0.88%	-0.06	15%	39	339	6	56	24
25	943,899	-1.15%	-0.09	12%	39	459	5	50	23
35	933,172	-1.37%	-0.13	11%	39	555	3	47	22
45	933,612	-1.36%	-0.14	10%	39	606	3	46	20
55	939,448	-1.24%	-0.15	9%	39	635	2	45	20

29th December 1993 to 28th December 1998

Max short instruments	Ending balance	CAGR (%)	Mar	Max total DD	Longest DD (mnth)	Trades	StdDev	Win duration	Loss duration
5	722,373	-6.30%	-0.17	37%	62	151	14	51	23
15	877,550	-2.58%	-0.12	22%	56	336	7	52	25
25	927,418	-1.50%	-0.1	15%	56	489	5	48	25
35	921,633	-1.62%	-0.12	14%	56	618	4	46	23
45	923,924	-1.57%	-0.14	11%	56	705	3	45	22
55	934,876	-1.34%	-0.14	10%	56	771	3	44	22

28th December 1998 to 27th December 2003

Max short instruments	Ending balance	CAGR (%)	Mar	Max total DD	Longest DD (mnth)	Trades	StdDev	Win duration	Loss duration
5	579,917	-10.32%	-0.22	47%	60	181	19	49	33
15	904,479	-1.99%	-0.07	29%	30	433	14	63	24
25	904,012	-2.00%	-0.08	26%	25	595	12	60	25
35	931,840	-1.40%	-0.07	22%	25	782	10	61	25
45	935,811	-1.32%	-0.07	19%	25	960	9	58	25
55	937,951	-1.27%	-0.07	17%	25	1119	9	56	24

27th December 2003 to 20th November 2008

Max short instruments	Ending balance	CAGR (%)	Mar	Max total DD	Longest DD (mnth)	Trades	StdDev	Win duration	Loss duration
5	994,265	-0.12%	0	33%	60	135	13	42	24
15	1,121,287	2.36%	0.1	23%	53	322	11	46	21
25	1,192,874	3.65%	0.22	17%	55	472	11	43	21
35	1,220,569	4.14%	0.28	15%	57	617	10	43	19
45	1,247,352	4.60%	0.37	13%	53	727	10	43	19
55	1,237,004	4.42%	0.39	12%	57	807	9	45	19

Summary

- **Portfolio concentration.** Rotating into the best performing 10 to 15 instruments each month reaps increased returns without the need for leverage.

- **Outperformance of the enhanced BBBO System.** The Momentum System outperformed the enhanced BBBO System on both an absolute and risk adjusted basis on most of the portfolios tested in this chapter.

- **Equally weighting equities and commodities.** Even greater returns were seen for the Momentum System using one combined portfolio giving equal weight to equities and commodities. This came at the cost of significantly higher drawdowns and volatility.

- **Robust.** Stepped parameter testing suggests that the Momentum System seems to be robust over different portfolios, parameter settings and time frames.

- **Short trading.** Testing suggests that little or no benefit accrues from the use of the Momentum System to engage in short trades.

Conclusion

A few concluding notes following from the testing carried out for this book.

Stock picking is a waste of time

Extensive research over many years has shown traditional actively managed funds and stock picking to be an expensive waste of time.

Cheap index tracking funds are the logical investor's instrument of choice. The buy-and-hold approach using index tracking funds is certain to produce returns over the long term superior to the great majority of actively managed funds.

Applying a system to index trackers

This book has demonstrated however, that the investor with the intelligence, time and inclination can achieve far better risk adjusted returns than can be achieved using a buy-and-hold approach by applying a simple long-term trend following system to index tracking funds.

Do mechanical systems work?

The validity of a systematic, mechanical approach to investment has been demonstrated both by extensive academic research and by the real-life track records of many fund managers who have achieved consistent success over many years.

Back-testing

The interested investor can gain further comfort as to the validly of the mechanical approach to investing by conducting rigorous back-testing over many years of data using sophisticated software available at reasonable cost. The process does not require genius or great literacy in either mathematics or computer programming. Your own trading will also, in time, hopefully give you full confidence in the quantitative approach to investment.

Recent hedge fund performance

The public should not be alarmed or deterred by the performance of the hedge fund industry as a whole during the current financial crisis: many of the problems have arisen through the excessive use of gearing. The decline seen in the main hedge fund indices over the past year is modest compared to the losses recorded by world equity indices and traditional, actively managed equity funds. In any event, many diversified trend following funds achieved significant positive returns in 2008.

Diversification over different asset classes

The addition of alternative asset classes is well within the reach of even the smallest investor thanks to the growth of exchange traded commodities and dedicated funds devoted to currencies, bonds and other areas of investment. The tests in this book have demonstrated that diversification over different asset classes can greatly reduce the volatility and risk of an investment programme. Investment across different and low correlated investments has, in the past at least, helped to smooth returns and to shorten the periods of drawdown.

Leverage

The use of leverage may well prove too costly for the smaller investor and in any event, the systems outlined in this book demonstrate that an increase in returns can be achieved without the use of gearing. Investors who want to explore the possibilities inherent in leverage should investigate the futures markets which offer leverage and a very wide range of instruments from stock indices and bonds to metals, energy and agricultural products. Various providers have launched geared ETFs and ETCs but these do not cover a very wide range of markets and are said not to have lived up to their promise.

Shorting

Trading short sounds like a good idea – the ability to profit from bear markets as well as bull markets is a most attractive option. In practice, shorting fully collateralised ETFs and ETCs using a long-term trend following system is likely to prove disappointing and of little benefit.

Where to go from here

If you are still unsure as to the validity of rule-based trading systems but would like to explore the topic further, then buy a few more books on the topic. Many of the books on offer concentrate on the futures markets but the same principles apply.

Study the many track records of successful trend followers which are freely available.

Above all, subscribe to a reliable data feed, invest in back-testing software and spend many, many hours experimenting with different systems and portfolios. Back-testing is not difficult but it does require time and effort, and the more you put in, as with every aspect of life, the greater the rewards will be.

Appendix

Data used

Start	Equis symbol	Description
01/01/1900	.DJI	Dow Jones Industrials
01/01/1976	.MIWO00000PUS	MSCI World USD

Portfolio 1: Stock indices for which dividend data collected

Start	Equis symbol	Description
04/01/1980	.SPX	S&P 500
08/01/1980	.TOPX	Tokyo Stock Price Index
07/01/1981	.TWII	Taiwan Stock Exchange Weighted Index
06/01/1982	.AORD	S&P ASX ALL ORD INDEX
06/01/1982	.HSI	Hang Seng Index
06/01/1982	.KLSE	KLSE Composite
02/07/1982	.FTAS	FTSE All Share Index
02/07/1982	.GSPTSE	S&P TSX Composite
05/01/1983	.AEX	Amsterdam SE EOE Index
06/05/1983	.KS11	Korea Composite Stock Price Index
03/08/1984	.SMSI	Madrid SE Index
09/08/1985	.WBKI	Vienna SE Boersekammer Index
02/10/1986	.OMXS30	Stockholm OMX Index
06/01/1988	.SSMI	Swiss Market Index
05/05/1988	.OMXH25	HEX25 Index
23/08/1988	.FCHI	CAC 40 Index
03/03/1989	.ISEQ	Irish Stock Exchange ISEQ Overall Index
03/01/1990	.BSESN	Bombay SE Sensex Index
21/12/1990	.SSEC	Shanghai SE Composite Index CNY
06/01/1992	.BFX	Brussels SE Bel 20 Index
05/01/1993	.MIB30	Milan SE MIB 30 Index
16/12/1993	.GDAXI	German SE XETRA DAX Index
26/04/1995	.MXX	Mexico Bolsa Index
26/11/1996	.BVSP	Sao Paulo SE Bovespa Index BRL
06/10/1997	.RTX	Vienna OTEOB Russian Traded Index $
15/02/1999	.SGDOW	Dow Jones Singapore Stock Index